Laruelle and Art

ALSO AVAILABLE FROM BLOOMSBURY

The Last Humanity: A New Ecological Science, François Laruelle
Capitalism's Holocaust of Animals, Katerina Kolozova
Art as Human Practice: An Aesthetics, Georg W. Bertram
Tintoretto's Difference: Deleuze, Diagrammatics and Art History,
Kamini Vellodi

Laruelle and Art

The Aesthetics of Non-Philosophy

JONATHAN FARDY

BLOOMSBURY ACADEMIC
LONDON • NEW YORK • OXFORD • NEW DELHI • SYDNEY

BLOOMSBURY ACADEMIC
Bloomsbury Publishing Plc
50 Bedford Square, London, WC1B 3DP, UK
1385 Broadway, New York, NY 10018, USA

BLOOMSBURY, BLOOMSBURY ACADEMIC and the Diana logo are trademarks
of Bloomsbury Publishing Plc

First published in Great Britain 2020

Cover design by Peter Somogyi
Cover image © runna10 / iStock

A catalogue record for this book is available from the British Library.

A catalog record for this book is available from the Library of Congress.

ISBN: HB: 978-1-3501-1472-2
PB: 978-1-3501-1473-9
ePDF: 978-1-3501-1471-5
eBook: 978-1-3501-1474-6

Typeset by Deanta Global Publishing Services, Chennai, India
Printed and bound in Great Britain

To find out more about our authors and books visit www.bloomsbury.com
and sign up for our newsletters.

Dedicated to a future for three

.

Contents

Figures

Preface

A book that purports to be about Laruelle and art, but discusses only seven artworks might arouse suspicion. But this book is not strictly concerned with art. Nor is it principally a book that aims to apply Laruelle's thought to art. To do that would position Laruelle's work as a *philosophy of art* and repeat the domination of art by philosophy that Laruelle's non-aesthetics rightly resists. Non-aesthetics, as the reader will learn, is a sub-practice of Laruelle's intellectual project, which he identifies as "non-philosophy" or "non-standard philosophy."

The distinction between "standard" philosophy and non-philosophy will be explained in detail in the first chapter. It suffices to say for now that non-philosophy seeks by a variety of means to resist the standard operations of thought determined by established philosophical practice. So, my effort to philosophically (or theoretically) explicate Laruelle is open to the charge of doing a standard philosophical explication of Laruelle's non-philosophical aesthetics or "non-aesthetics." I plead no contest. But I would also nuance that charge. I have attempted to write a meta-philosophical analysis of the *aesthetics of non-aesthetics* or *the aesthetics of non-philosophy*. My thesis is: Laruelle's practice of non-philosophy is fundamentally an *aesthetic practice* even while it is not reducible to aesthetics as defined in the standard sense. Of central concern in the writing of this book has been the *style* of Laruelle's writing.

Style has an odd place in the history of philosophy. There are certainly philosophers who are famous for the style of their writing, good and bad. Many agree, for example, that Nietzsche was a great philosopher and great stylist. Some would agree that Hegel was a great philosopher and a terrible stylist. And many on first reading Laruelle might surmise that he was a terrible stylist and a confusing philosopher. Style and content in philosophical or theoretical writing has an asymmetrical relation as compared to the field of literature. Literary scholars differ on the importance of style and content (or content and form) and they differ as to how to theorize that relation.

But there is general agreement that literary "content" cannot be easily distinguished from the "form" in which it is presented. But that is not how many philosophers think. A simple anecdote from my own experience testifies to this. The first year of my doctoral studies, I joined a student-run reading group whose aim was to read *Capital* by Marx. We agreed to read the book together and to meet and discuss it once a week. The meeting opened each time with a student giving a presentation on that week's reading. My turn came up. I started out by saying that I wanted to focus on the metaphors that Marx used in the section we read. I was abruptly cut-off midstream by a self-proclaimed "Marxist" who informed me that reading *Capital* in a "literary" way was wrong. The point he insisted was to read *Capital* "philosophically." That argument didn't convince me, especially since Marx makes many references to literature throughout *Capital*. But I didn't have a good argument as to why his thinking was wrongheaded.

I have always had a certain interest in the style of philosophy or theory. My reading of theory began in strange wonder at words by Derrida, Althusser, Baudrillard, Benjamin, Adorno, and so on. I came to theory through the disciplinary paths of art history and visual culture. And in these fields, the question of style is a profound *theoretical* problem. Indeed, the modern practice of art history was founded in the attempt to categorize and taxonomize art-historical styles. But as I ventured forth in my study of "theory and criticism" as a doctoral student, I found that this problem of style seemed to vanish in seminars that delved into "ideas." Discussion of rhetoric was largely confined to "theories of rhetoric," but the *rhetoric of theory* was very rarely considered. Even deconstruction's concern with rhetoric and figural language was largely contained by teaching it as a *theory*. The whole question of style seemed to be quarantined by well-meaning professors. It must be said that the rigorous way in which theorists read theory is valuable. It holds theories accountable for their claims. But it is also the case that the reticence to read theory rhetorically is a defense mechanism. Analytic philosophers often impugn theory (or Continental philosophy) for being merely "rhetorical" or worse mere "sophistry." Thus, the response by some theorists is to prove their philosophical mettle by sidelining the question of style in the name of expounding ideas. I experienced this quite personally during my doctoral studies at the Centre for Theory and Criticism. My department was located across the street from a leading analytic philosophy department. Theory and philosophy students tended to regard each other with a mixture of indifference and disdain. The feud was a feud in the classic sense as its passion was only matched by the obscurity of the cause for that passion. The feud exists for the sake of aggrandizing the stakes of either side. But, at its heart, the feud has much to do with an argument over the use of language in critical discourse. The feud is largely a feud over style.

I must say that on first reading Laruelle I was put off by his style even while I was used to reading quite "obscure" prose by that point. But I was even more put off by his "non-philosophy." Where was the argument? Why these axioms? Why does he reduce philosophy to "Philosophical Decision?" What's so bad about philosophy? Who's he to say what philosophy is in the first place? Isn't Laruelle doing philosophy? What's the difference between non-philosophy and anti-philosophy? Is this a new theory of metaphilosophy? If this isn't philosophy, why does it seem to be all about philosophy? It was all a bit of a surprise and surprisingly disconcerting to find myself impugning Laruelle for not being "philosophical" enough. My arguments with Laruelle scholars and enthusiasts seemed to force myself uncomfortably into a position a little too close to that typically assumed by those on the "analytic" side of the philosophy/theory feud. The problem, I think, is that I came to Laruelle with a little *too much* theory. I discovered him late in my graduate study with a good deal of standard theoretical reading behind me. What seemed to be happening, without me being fully aware of it, was an uncomfortable return to what once had been exhilarating: the wonder at words I found difficult to understand. It would take time for me to read Laruelle with that pleasure that led me to read theory in the first place.

Reading Laruelle became more natural the more it became more "rhetorical." And by that form of reading, the theory of non-philosophy began to make more sense. These two facets of Laruelle—rhetorical and theoretical—radically intersect in his elaboration of non-standard aesthetics or "non-aesthetics." What Laruelle says, and how he says it, works together in a symbiotic way. Laruelle's "method" (if this is the right word) is to "clone" theory or philosophy by rendering it in a rhetorical and syntactical form that is ultimately faithful to Laruelle's most radical axiom: the epistemic foreclosure of the "Real."[1]

This book will unpack this axiomatic claim concerning the Real in more detail, but to put the matter simply here: Laruelle axiomatically insists that the Real is radical immanence itself. The Real is radical immanence itself of which thought itself is a part. There can be no final philosophy "of" the Real in the strict sense for every philosophy is immanent to the Real. There is no position or place exterior to the Real from which any thought (philosophical or not) can survey and grasp the Real. This first axiom of non-philosophy largely explains why Laruelle's writing is full of strange and sometimes awkward syntactical and rhetorical constructions. Laruelle tries to think in a radically immanent manner that will not reproduce the illusions of standard philosophy by defaulting into a philosophy "of" or "on" the Real. Standard philosophy, by contrast, is marked by this decision on the Real. It is this decision that Laruelle names "Philosophical Decision."[2] The non-standard method consists in "cloning" philosophy or theory to render philosophies as "raw materials" voided of their decisional character. Non-philosophy is firstly an effort to *immanentize* philosophy.

I say all this not to jump the gun on Chapter 1, but to make clear my thesis concerning what is at stake in the *aesthetics of Laruelle's writings on non-aesthetics*. The standard distinctions between fields like art and aesthetics have no impact on the Real, which for Laruelle is "One" and irreducible to any distinctions for all distinctions are immanent to it. This means that for Laruelle we should re-present the relation between art and aesthetics (or art and philosophy) in a "non-relational" presentation. From the perspective of the Real as One, or what Laruelle calls "vision-in-One," there is no "relation" for there is no relation "in" the Real since the Real encompasses all relations. That is why, as Laruelle has said repeatedly, he is a "realist" in theory inasmuch as he tries to realistically follow out the consequences of his grounding axiom. This means adopting a certain *style of writing* that approximates what he calls an "art-thought" that *aesthetically thinks aesthetics* in a non-dialectical, non-dominating, non-standard way. As Laruelle explains in an interview:

It is important to understand that non-philosophy is that-which-I-do-in-saying and not just what I say, which could always be taken hold of again by philosophy. It is what I do with the language of philosophy and "from" this language. We don't have to project an image of non-philosophy into some new heaven—a Platonic one, for example. Non-philosophy is a practice and an immanent practice. This is what screens out a lot of philosophers, because philosophers always project something or desire it. I don't have a desire for the Real.[3]

Laruelle's practice of non-aesthetics signals an irreducibly aesthetic moment immanent to philosophy, theory, and non-philosophy alike. There is always a moment of "how" in writing that is "superposed" with "what." And if traditional philosophers have tended to set the "how" aside in the name of the "what" that is itself no reason to ignore it. This is not a radically new insight by any means. Many writers on the arts, including figures such as Theodor Adorno, Walter Benjamin, and Jacques Derrida (who are the focus of Chapter 2), self-consciously adopted styles of writing that they considered proper for the art that they took seriously.

However, what is unique about Laruelle's approach is that he makes this aesthetic dimension rhetorically and methodologically explicit through a set of "fictional" strategies. But as I show, it is not simply that Laruelle makes philosophy *look* like literature, art, or "fiction" in the broadest sense. There is something more fundamental going on. He does not merely "invert" the traditional prioritization that places art under the authority of philosophy for he is no dialectician. Rather, Laruelle's work *deprioritizes prioritization* itself via his axiomatic insistence on the radically unified immanence of the Real. The "distinction" between art and philosophy, upon which standard aesthetic schemas of prioritization are founded, is neutralized by Laruelle's radical perspective of "vision-in-One." His "fictions" are "conjugations" of philosophical and artistic raw materials. But Laruelle's fictions do not simply "blend" or "mix" art and philosophy. Laruelle is suspicious of amphibological strategies of mixing for they negatively preserve the principle of distinctions in the very concept of "mixture." Laruelle's fictions of art aim to escape amphibological blending or dialectical contrasting for a "superposing" of art and philosophy. Laruelle's "art-fictions" seek out the "hypothesis" in art. He asks: How does the artwork think? And how can art open a new way of thinking not only art, but philosophy, politics, ethics, and so forth? "Art-thought" for Laruelle is more than the simplistic and patronizing gesture of giving "philosophical credit" to art. It credits the radical thesis that philosophy is immanently and inescapably aesthetic. I see Laruelle's theoretical fictions as the playing out of this radical thesis.

Aim

The aim of this book is to contextualize and interrogate Laruelle's immanently aesthetic practice of non-aesthetics and to show the ethical and political dimensions immanent to that practice. The aim is to show how Laruelle's work is less strange than it might at first seem by showing its similarities with well-established patterns of "modernist" and "postmodernist" theory. Laruelle's non-aesthetics circumvents the dialectical trap of subordinating thought to art or art to thought by "conjugating" or "superposing" the two. Non-aesthetics breaks with the representationalist metaphysics of reflection. Rather than reflecting on art, Laruelle introjects art into philosophy by "cloning" it. Art enters the field of non-aesthetic practice not in the form of explication but as a *performative aesthetic practice* for thinking otherwise than art or philosophy as conceived in the "standard" sense.

Outline of Chapters

Chapter 1 provides an introduction to the basic terms and core axioms of non-philosophy of which non-aesthetics is one form. Key concepts and terms are explained, including the Real, Philosophical Decision, Principle of Sufficient Philosophy, and standard philosophy. It also offers a brief overview of the roots of Laruelle's project as he himself has historicized it. This personal history gives us the means to understand the origins of Laruelle's aesthetic of non-philosophy.

The chapter further examines Laruelle's place in a tradition of thought that Richard Rorty describes as the view that philosophy is a "kind of writing." This view accepts as given that philosophy is a genre of writing whose profile is drawn from a variety of writerly models including fiction and literature broadly. It moves on to draw connections between Laruelle's knowingly naïve concept of concrete human life and the victimization of the human and art at the hands of standard philosophy. Philosophy victimizes art, as it does concrete human life, by turning them into abstract concepts subordinate to philosophical reason. What Laruelle seeks is not a philosophy of art nor the human, but a human (and humane) *art of philosophy*. The chapter interrogates this question of the art of philosophy by examining the parallel case of Marcel Duchamp's readymade philosophical art. I argue that what is common to the case of Duchamp and Laruelle is the problem of reading. How to *read non-philosophy non-philosophically* parallels the problem of how to read Duchamp's challenge to the primacy of originality without reducing that challenge itself to an original vision in conformity with the standard humanist practice of art history. The chapter concludes with an examination and exploration of the role that style and "science" plays in the practice of non-philosophy.

Chapter 2 examines the "non" of non-philosophy and by extension that of non-aesthetics. The chapter opens with a meditation on the "unfocused" work of the pioneering nineteenth-century photographer, Julia Margaret Cameron. Her work instituted a new conception of focus that broke the binary of "in-focus" versus "out-of-focus." Her "soft-focused" work proposed a new axiomatic for photographic practice that demonstrated that the aesthetic of sharp focus was simply a naturalized convention. I draw a parallel between Cameron's work in photography and Laruelle's in philosophy. It is not that Cameron negates sharp focus nor that Laruelle negates philosophy. Rather, both perform an "art of negation" that negates negation in the standard sense. They instate a new axiomatic that brings into view the fact that standardized and naturalized ways of working in photography and philosophy are simply a set of conventions that normalize philosophical and photographic practice. The chapter continues with the theme of focus via an examination of the focus of non-aesthetics. It contextualizes Laruelle's aestheticized approach to aesthetics by framing his work in relation to a constellation of modernist and postmodernist thinkers such as Theodor Adorno, Walter Benjamin, and Jacques Derrida. These thinkers seek to find a measure of interplay *between art and the art of writing on it*. The paratactic tenor of Adorno's writing paralleled his sense of the autonomy of modernist works of art; Benjamin's surrealistically juxtaposed "dialectical images" parallels the revolutionary surrealist art of montage and collage; Derrida's creative practice of criticism carves out a creative freedom for criticism. All these writerly thinkers broke the mirror of representationalist criticism. This break parallels the radical break with representation that erupted with the emergence of the avant-gardes in the early twentieth century to which Adorno, Benjamin, and Derrida creatively and critically responded.

However, what distinguishes Laruelle's *aesthetic practice of non-aesthetics* is the implicit theory underlying it that may be stated as the hypothesis concerning the *irreducibly aesthetic nature of philosophical practice itself*. The chapter then examines the role of "fiction" and its relationship to "cloning" in Laruelle's work. The analysis intersects with an examination of Laruelle's theoretical work on photography (or non-photography). Fiction, like photographic images, is understood by Laruelle to have its own immanent reality parallel to that of the Real. Laruelle takes the Real to be immanent and non-relational for it encompasses all relations. Thus, his "fictions" are realistic with respect to the Real in that they "clone" the *non-relationality of the Real* into their very structure and syntax. Finally, the chapter concludes with a brief introduction to Laruelle's "matrixial mechanics," a method by which art and philosophy are "matrixed" in order to produce an object for theory that cannot be reduced to art or philosophy. This section helps prepare the way for an exploration of the aesthetics of Laruelle's quantum "science fiction."

Chapter 3 begins with an examination of Michael Frayn's Tony Award–winning play, *Copenhagen*. The play is based on a real historical event. In 1941, Werner Heisenberg travelled by train from Germany to Denmark to visit his mentor, Niels Bohr. The meeting was fraught. Heisenberg was at the center of physics in a country that was quickly coming to dominate the whole of Europe. Denmark was already under occupation. No one, including Heisenberg and Bohr, could ever agree as to what precisely was discussed. What is certain is that it marked the end of nearly twenty years of friendship. Frayn's play is structured by a fictional representation of the "uncertainty relations" that govern atomic interactions to metaphorically represent the "uncertain relations" between the characters and a series of "chain reactions" that just might have prevented Hitler from getting the bomb. Frayn's play explores what he calls "quantum ethics."

Frayn's play provides a useful inroad to discuss Laruelle's fictive use of quantum theory in his elaboration of non-aesthetics. The chapter also examines Laruelle's critique of the standard conception of light as "truth" in the standard tradition. Laruelle's creative photo-fiction is an attempt to rewrite "photo-graphy"—light-writing—as "light-fiction" and this intersects profoundly with his "science fiction" work insofar as it constitutes a fictive use of the science of light. I am particularly concerned with how Laruelle conjugates the aesthetic and the scientific (in his sense) into the matrix of non-aesthetic practice. The chapter further explores the ethical and political dimensions of Laruelle's "science fiction" through an examination of his engagement with Marx and Marxism. I conclude with a discussion of "fractality" in Laruelle's discussion of photography and his ethics of the human as a matrixed measure against essentialism, but not against universality.

Chapter 4 argues that despite non-philosophy's resistance to Philosophical Decision it should be conceptualized as a *decision against deciding* on the Real or what I call "non-philosophical decisionism." This decisionism at the heart of non-philosophy proves decisive for doing non-aesthetics as I show through three case studies in the art of light: Anish Kapoor, Dan Flavin, and James Turrell.

The work of each of these artists forces criticism into a state of crisis for in each case it appears that the criticality of the artwork reduces the critical response to a double, mime, or clone of the artwork. I show what can be done in and through this critical condition of cloning via non-aesthetic strategies. Kapoor forces open the problem of "reflection," Flavin forces open the problem of history, and Turrell forces open the dialectic of truth and illusion. These crises in criticism are placed into dialogue with Benjamin's concept of the "angle of vision," which provides a measure for thinking Laruelle's non-dialectical recasting of art and philosophy as a *relation of non-relation* or what Benjamin might call "dialectics at a standstill."

The chapter concludes by thinking this *non-relation of the relation of art to philosophy* in light of Laruelle's radicalization of Louis Althusser's thesis of the "last instance." Laruelle holds that the relation between art and philosophy (and all other fields) is non-relational when seen from the perspective of the radical immanence of the Real or "vision-in-One." Laruelle's consistent axiom is that the Real is foreclosed to full epistemic access, but it is determinant in the last instance for knowledge. The concept of the last instance, or "determination-in-the-last instance," to be precise, occupies a fascinating place in non-philosophy as it is both a theory and an object of non-philosophical theory. The chapter concludes by asking the question: To what extent is non-aesthetics a theory? There is then a short concluding chapter that briefly reviews the basic arguments of the book and indicates directions for future research.

Hope

My hope is that this book will help clarify Laruelle's thought for the uninitiated and the more experienced reader. Particularly, I hope that this book will encourage you to read Laruelle's work and find useful or interesting ways to do so. Finally, my hope is that this book helps make the case for why art historians, art theorists, and artists should read Laruelle's work. The time for new theory is now. Laruelle's work provides us with another narrative of so-called "French Theory" of a very different kind than that grouped under "philosophies of difference." It gives us an alternate way to think in terms of unification, universalization, and unilateralism without lapsing into uncritical and repressive thought. Laruelle gives us tools to think art in ways that remind us of what makes art so powerful and fascinating: its capacity to think thought in radically new ways.

Acknowledgments

I want to start by thanking my wife, Amy Wuest, PhD, whose patience, encouragement, and incisive criticism have been vital to this project. I want to also thank my colleagues in the Department of Art at Idaho State University for their support of my work and career. I would also be remiss if I didn't thank all my students who continue to push my thought. I am especially grateful to the graduate students who gave up a Wednesday evening every two weeks to read theory and listen to me ramble on. Also, I am thankful to all the many great Laruelle scholars out there, many of whom appear in my notes. I could not have written this without their work. Finally, I want to thank my editor, Liza Thompson, for her steadfast support for this project.

1

Introduction

This introductory chapter briefly situates Laruelle within postwar Continental philosophy and introduces the key concepts of non-philosophy and non-aesthetics. It explores what the implications of non-philosophy are for the practice of aesthetics in a non-philosophical register. Of principal concern will be examining the following terms: Real, Philosophical Decision, Principle of Sufficient Philosophy, and "generic science." Along the way, we will draw parallels with the visual and literary arts as well as various philosophical traditions that have played a key role in the development of Laruelle's non-philosophical project. This is a long chapter. But its aim is to sufficiently situate non-philosophy in order to prepare the way for an explication of non-aesthetics.

The real problem

John O' Maoilearca astutely points out that introducing any reader to the thought of Laruelle presents very real problems.[1] Why? Because there is hardly any way to do so without making his non-philosophy sound suspiciously like standard philosophy. Already we have said quite a bit. First, non-philosophy is not a negation of philosophy or "standard philosophy." This is why Laruelle's later adoption of the term "non-standard philosophy" is less misleading than his older (but more used) "non-philosophy." Whatever else non-philosophy may be, it is not a standard practice of philosophical thought. But this begs the question: What is "standard philosophy"? Much of this book will be concerned with that question in one form or another. But suffice to say that Laruelle has consistently argued that standard philosophical practice is chiefly concerned with determining what the Real is. This naturally begs another question: What is the Real? Readers of Jacques Lacan might find an initial foothold here. Lacan used this term throughout his tortuous prose. The French postwar psychoanalyst's sense of the Real is not wholly dissimilar from Laruelle's. Lacan understood the Real as that which resists symbolization. In other words, the Real is that which cannot be put into language (or symbolic form of any kind). The Real for Lacan is thus what cannot be assimilated into knowledge.

Laruelle's sense of the Real reworks the "raw material" of Lacan's concept and reformats it.[2] Laruelle retains Lacan's notion of the Real as something that cannot be conceptualized or reduced to symbolic reference. What he jettisons, however, is Lacan's claim that the Real is trauma. The Lacanian Real is determined by a human-centric conceptualization as experience that resists human intelligibility. But for Laruelle, the Real cannot be even negatively subsumed by any human-centric concept—trauma or otherwise. The Real for Laruelle does not only resist human modes of symbolic representation (like language); it resists all modes of conceptualization. The Real is not only foreclosed to symbolization; it is foreclosed to all forms of thought including psychoanalysis and philosophy. Katerina Kolozova explicates the Laruellean Real precisely:

> In non-philosophy (also called non-standard philosophy), the "real" is the instance of [a] unilateral, indifferent, effect of a radical exteriority with respect to the signifying subject. In other words, one does not refer to the abstraction of "the Real," but rather to concrete instances of an effect of the real, of that which always already escapes signification but is nonetheless out there.[3]

The Real for Laruelle is "out there" but all we can epistemically access are limited, partial, and local "effects" of the Real. And even "effects" has to be placed in scare quotes for it is a displaced name. What appears to be an effect of the Real only appears as such because of the schismatic forcing of causal relations (cause and effect), but which are in the last instance unilaterally determined by the Real as One.

Philosophical Decision is a constant motif in all Laruelle's texts. It is always capitalized because for Laruelle it is the proper name for a gesture repeated ad-infinitum by standard philosophy. All standard philosophies decide on the Real. They make a decision concerning what the Real is. The Real, for Lacan, as noted is trauma. But every standard philosophy has its own version of the Real. The Real for Plato was the world of perfect truths—the Forms. The Real for Heidegger was that of Being itself. The Real for Foucault was "discourse" and its power-effects. Every philosophy, argues Laruelle, decides on the Real and this decision organizes its discourse and prescribes a hierarchy of concepts. Philosophical Decision is established on the basis of a governing presupposition: philosophy is sufficient to know or decide the Real. It is this presupposition that Laruelle names "Principle of Sufficient Philosophy."

Non-philosophy begins from a different axiom: the Real is foreclosed to thought. It is foreclosed to thought for it is radical immanence. The all that is cannot be reduced to a single concept or even a multiplicity of concepts. There is no way to think the Real immanently without representing it partly, which is to represent it falsely. Furthermore, any attempt to represent the Real unavoidably limits itself by determining or deciding that the Real is a matter of representation, or its dialectical double, the unrepresentable. The Real for Laruelle is not a concept for it cannot be subsumed within a schema of representational or non-representational thought. Non-philosophy is thus committed to a radically immanent conception of the Real: the Real is that which is immanence itself. Alex Dubilet notes that non-philosophy does not "take immanence as its object, its result, or even its milieu, but as the foreclosed Real."[4] Non-philosophy is thus radically distinct from standard philosophies of immanence.

Postwar thought has been committed to dispensing with metaphysical and transcendental categories and organizing systems. Philosophies of immanence have dispensed with Truth, Man, History, Meaning, Totality, and Universality in the name of immanent and fragmented multiplicities of truth-claims and knowledge practices. This perspective links the very different projects of Gilles Deleuze and Félix Guattari, Jacques Derrida, Luce Irigaray, Gayatri Chakravorty Spivak, Judith Butler, and so many others. This laudable effort to decenter, de-privilege, and deconstruct unquestioned transcendental signifieds marked an important step in "overcoming metaphysics." Postwar theory sought to think from difference as the immanent condition of the Real. But for Laruelle, standard philosophies of immanence erred in *transcendentalizing immanence* (and difference) by placing the Real under the sign of radical difference.

Contrastingly, non-philosophy "is presented as an immanent thought," writes John Mullarkey, "precisely *because* it does not try to think of the Real but only alongside it or 'according to' it."[5] Mullarkey's key phrase "according to" indexes the affinity that Laruelle's thought shares with the phenomenological tradition. It was Edmund Husserl, the founder of phenomenology, who called for a philosophy of phenomena that would be attentive to the *reality of appearance as appearance*. Husserl's method of philosophizing "brackets" out the question of the Real when investigating phenomenal experience. The bracketing procedure—the *epoché*—in Husserl's system is "cloned" in Laruelle's work. But he radicalizes it by "bracketing" not only the Real from reflection but also Husserl's decisional split between appearance and the Real in one stroke. We will see many such "clones" of philosophical concepts in Laruelle's work, for non-philosophy is not a break with philosophy; it is a mutation. Laruelle trained as a philosopher and this training marked his thought. But he has sought to rethink how to use philosophy. Most importantly he has attempted to do philosophy the way an artist does art: by assembling "raw materials" into new constructions. But his work should not be thought of as simply another instance of the eclecticizing procedures of postmodern theorizing whose master form is the bricolage. Indeed, Laruelle is explicitly against that "anything goes" approach. Laruelle's work is axiomatically faithful to a core metaphysical principle: the Real is foreclosed to full epistemic access. And Laruelle's style of non-philosophy (as we will see) is determined by that metaphysical axiom. It is useful, then, to examine Laruelle's path to non-philosophy in order to better situate his thought in relation to his peers.

Toward non-philosophy

Laruelle divides his work into five periods: Philosophy I (1971–81), Philosophy II (1981–95), Philosophy III (1995–2002), Philosophy IV (2002–08), and Philosophy V (2008–present). His work early on sought to find a radically immanent route to transcendental thought. But by his own estimation it was not until the third period that he began to pursue a path that he hoped would transcend philosophy itself.

Laruelle chose to study philosophy with some reservation. But the reservation had to do with what *kind of writing* he wanted to study. He found himself for a moment in a state of indecision between the choice to study literature or philosophy. So, the first *decision* he found he had to make was the decision between philosophy and literature. He chose the former, but the place of the literary, especially fiction, within the philosophical has haunted his work ever since. As Laruelle notes:

> I can't speak of any special experience that drove me into philosophy. I found myself in a class where I did a year of philosophy, before I chose to continue it—but I remember that I hesitated for some time over whether to study literature or philosophy. In the end, I chose the latter, and it went very well. But I always used to write very "literary" texts about philosophy.[6]

He was to go on to write a thesis under the influence of Michel Henry titled *The Absence of Being*. His decision on this particular philosophical theme was in part inspired by film. Recalling his decision, Laruelle notes: "I came back from vacation, having seen Antonioni's *La Notte*, and I told my supervisor, Paul Ricoeur, that I renounced Hegel! . . . So yes, that film was also a turning point, curious things like that happen."[7]

Precisely how Antonioni's film about the breakdown of a marriage impacted Laruelle's decision against Hegel is hard to say. Perhaps philosophy is always, as its name indicates, a kind of love. Readers and students fall in love (and out of love) with philosophers. Some texts seduce and others leave us cold. Richard Rorty reminds us in his essay on Jacques Derrida that philosophy is a form of writing. Excluding some militant purists, most people get into philosophy for rather "un-philosophical" reasons. If we are honest with ourselves, says Rorty, we will admit that our reasons for reading certain philosophers rather than others often has less to do with the relative strengths of their arguments or even their relevancy. We read certain philosophers because they attract us. And they attract us through their words—through writing. But while we know that the way philosophers write plays a non-trivial role in why they are read, this is not often how they are taught to students. We teach students to value philosophers for their *ideas*. We tend not to use the word "writer" when referring to a philosopher.

It was philosophy's bias against writing that Derrida marshaled his creative efforts against. This surely explains why Laruelle was attracted to his work early on. The "writerly" or "literary" quality of Derrida's texts—a quality noted by both his champions and critics—represents, for Rorty, the self-conscious acceptance by Derrida that philosophy is a "kind of writing." In Rorty's view, Derrida's work is at its best when it is at its most "literary." This is the Derrida of the late 1970s and early 1980s, just after he consolidated his theory (or "science") of writing, his "grammatology," and just before his "ethical turn." This period is marked by his most experimental texts, notably *Glas*, which features two columns of text contrasting Hegel's writings on the family with those of the novelist Jean Genet. The text is a study in (among other things) the collision or conflict between philosophy and literature. Derrida's commentary runs between the two columns seeking in some measure to transcend the division without resolving it via a theoretical synthesis in the spirit of philosophy or a narrative in the spirit of literature. Rorty writes:

> To get a handle on his [Derrida's] work, one might take him as answering the question, "Given that philosophy *is* a kind of writing, why does this suggestion meet with such resistance?" This becomes, in his work, the slightly more particular question, "What must philosophers who object to this characterization think *writing* is, that they should find the notion that that is what they are doing so offensive?"[8]

Laruelle affirms Rorty and Derrida's critique of philosophy's anti-literary bias. Standard philosophy likes to think of itself as relatively free from "literary" and "rhetorical" concerns. This standard bias is but the latest manifestation of classical philosophy's suspicion of the arts. The denunciation of "sophistry" ranges across philosophical history from Plato to Quine. Today, the mantle of suspicion has been passed to many self-identified "analytic" philosophers who like to distinguish themselves from those working in the "humanities." Philosophers work on hard "analytical" problems: rational deduction, logic, science, language. They teach others how to think "critically." It all sounds good, especially to penny-pinching university administrators who are eager to defund any and all forms of study whose pre-professional economic value cannot be easily determined. And because art is always on the "chopping block" and the sciences always on the rise, standard philosophy has sought to save itself by demonstrating its "scientific" character. Standard philosophy cannot—heaven forbid—countenance the fact that philosophy and art are both products of culture nor that each contains an irreducibly aesthetic dimension.

Laruelle and Derrida, by contrast, founded forms of theory that embrace its aesthetic character. Their work in different ways articulate ways of doing philosophy as a "kind of writing." This in each case resulted in forms of writing that are simply neither "literary" nor "philosophical" in the standard sense. This development had a close parallel in the visual arts. At the very moment that thinkers like Derrida and Laruelle were challenging the established genre boundaries of philosophical writing, visual artists were challenging the standard boundaries between diverse media. The discrete medial identity of painting, sculpture, and architecture was challenged by boundary crossing practices and "mixed-media" strategies. One of the pioneers of this was the American artist, Robert Rauschenberg (1925–2008) (Figure 1).

Rauschenberg emerged in the mid-1950s in the twilight of American Abstract Expressionism. He voided that heroic movement of its philosophy of radical individuality and emotional expressivity. Rauschenberg took the visual grammar of Abstract Expressionism—expressive color and violent brushstrokes—and reduced it to the status of raw material on par with any other "found" thing. Tires, stuffed animals, crushed cans, rusted bathtubs, photocopies of artworks, clippings from the sports pages, astronauts, Kennedy, the rich and famous, the unknown—all found their way into Rauschenberg's

FIGURE 1 *Robert Rauschenberg,* Reservoir, *1961.*

Source: Oil, pencil, fabric, wood, and metal on canvas with two electric clocks, rubber tread wheel, and spoked wheel rim 85 1/2 × 62 1/2 × 15 1/2 inches (217.2 × 158.8 × 39.4 cm). Smithsonian American Art Museum, Washington, D.C. Gift of S.C. Johnson & Son, Inc. © Robert Rauschenberg Foundation / VAGA at Artists Rights Society (ARS), NY.

"combines." His surfaces slathered with the faded detritus of high and low culture extend beyond two dimensions, creating sites and environments that challenge the medial distinctions between painting, sculpture, and architecture as they had been established in standard "modernist" practice. He made his "combines" by collecting raw materials on his walks around his studio in New York. Rauschenberg's walks established a process for letting the world back into the rarefied space of abstract art. The sanctity of pure form was creatively negated by a philosophical flat-lining of distinctions between high and low and between medial borders. The fact that Rauschenberg's combines were controversial at the time is telling. Rauschenberg's combines voided the medial and material distinctions between two-dimensional and three-dimensional space (as well as high and low culture) and created a new aesthetic matrix from these raw materials and medial borders.

Rauschenberg's practice let the great outside back into art by practically destroying the philosophical boundary between art and the everyday as Marcel Duchamp had done before him. Rauschenberg took Duchamp's thought and reworked it to strategically target the ideological divisions between specific media. His surfaces filled with accumulations of visual and material culture *de-defined* the delimiting parameters between art and the everyday ramified and reinforced by the rhetoric of high modernist philosophy and formalist criticism. Rauschenberg's art suggests a "ceaseless inflow" of "message, stimulus, and impediment" in the words of Leo Steinberg.[9] Rauschenberg redefined "surface" as it had been philosophized in the modernist practice of aesthetics. The modernist "surface" was the hallowed surface of high art. Rauschenberg's work sought to make that rarefied "surface" into the plane of the real world in all its messiness. Art, for Rauschenberg, was no longer to exist in the vacuum of the studio but was to expand to the streets outside. He leveled the surface of art down to the surfaces of the everyday. Rauschenberg's "postmodernist" surface was transformed into a surface "to which anything reachable-thinkable would adhere. It had to be whatever a billboard or dashboard is, and everything a projection screen is, with further affinities for anything that is flat and worked over—palimpsest."[10]

Like the assemblage art of Rauschenberg, the textual play of Laruelle and Derrida's "experimental" or non-standard texts are like tableaus of accumulated and palimpsestic fragments. Logical perspective, linearity, strict geometrical connections are abandoned for a mode of working that lets the world back into philosophy. Rather than decide on philosophy or literature, Laruelle's trajectory traces out (in a somewhat Derridean or Rauschenbergian fashion) an effort to open philosophy up to the suppressed "outside" of writing, literature, and "fiction."

Philosophy's great outside—art, music, politics, life—has been, and continues to be, decisive for Laruelle's thought. But, rather than allow his work to become a philosophy of art, or a "standard aesthetics" in his terms, Laruelle allows art to determine or decide his theoretical work. He seeks not a philosophy of art or aesthetics, but an aesthetics or an *art of philosophy*. The critical mimesis that Laruelle produces does not take the form of a philosophical reflection *on* art. His is a critical mimeticism in reverse. Like Rauschenberg's surfaces, Laruelle's non-philosophical foundation is a combine of sorts or what he calls a "matrix." The matrix—a term he clones from quantum physics—is a "surface" on which he combines and collides diverse materials from science, art, and philosophy in order to produce a form of "fiction" that is irreducible to any of its material sources. As Laruelle puts it in *Photo-Fiction*

> The artist of philo[sophical]-fiction that refers to the photo, to the painting, or to music, knows how to stop at this insurrectional and creative plane of art, creative precisely because its most dominant [philosophical] finalities are taken out of play. . . . As if the spontaneous and doxic relief of thinking was annihilated and resurrected by an insurrectional subtraction of words.[11]

Laruelle's creative and insurrectional use of language (quantic and otherwise) aims at a radical subtraction of the exalted surfaces of high "relief" philosophy. Like the art of bas-relief sculpture, Laruelle seeks to level down the surface of philosophy. No longer a surface over which it orders the things of the world—"the order of things" in Foucault's words—Laruelle opens the philosophical tableau to the trace of art and aesthetics: the philosopher as stenographer of art rather than its judge and jury. "One day, after I had completed my studies," Laruelle recalls, "I sat at my desk; and I cleared away all the books, everything that had already been written. I started again with a new blank sheet of paper, and I began to search myself."[12]

What was Laruelle searching for? Even then, he was looking for a way to transcend, or at least get over, philosophy. The freedom imagined in the tabula rasa—the clearing away of books and the trappings of schooldays—and the confrontation with the stubbornness of a blank page offers an irresistibly fitting metaphor for the work of non-philosophy. But the "non" of "non-philosophy" is not negation. One does not escape philosophy by ceasing to read. Laruelle notes:

> Of course it's not necessary to read philosophy to philosophize, just as it's not necessary to go to church to be a believer. More exactly, even if one does not professionally, dogmatically, "do philosophy," all of the vocabulary of more or less general notions one uses is philosophizable.[13]

Laruelle came to see that "extent philosophy is truly immense" for it encompasses not only libraries but is, of course, reflected in the very concepts we use to think.[14] We are, most of us, already doing philosophy by thinking with philosophical concepts even though most of us don't recognize it. William James in his remarkable lectures on pragmatism argued something similar. James held that philosophical "schools" are really just formalizations of human "temperaments" shaped by the cultural diffusion of philosophy.[15] We are all, at one time or another, empiricists, idealists, rationalists, and so forth. We may never use those terms, but our "temperaments" are marked by the features of those schools of thought. So, even if one stops reading philosophy, the work of philosophy on our temperaments continues. And this spontaneous philosophy—what might be called a *philosophical unconscious*—is harder still to get clear of for it structures one's thought unconsciously. Clearing away the philosophy books does not get one clear of philosophy. Nor, it must be said, was this Laruelle's aim.

Non-philosophy does not begin with the abstract. It is radically concrete in its orientation despite its strange syntax and seemingly abstract, even abstruse, language. Non-philosophy begins by turning the philosophy of the "hermeneutics of suspicion" back upon philosophy itself. Non-philosophy is radically suspicious about the claims of philosophy. Above all, it refuses to simply accept that philosophy is sufficient to know or decide upon the Real. Non-philosophy's radically immanent perspective rejects out-of-hand the idea that there is any place external to the immanence of the Real from which philosophy can establish an authoritative perspective over the Real. This is a radically simple, even naïve, point of view. But it is also quite realistic and pragmatic. It is from this naïve and finite perspective that Laruelle proceeds. Non-philosophy will not decide the Real and thus it will also not decide which school of philosophy is right. Rather it democratizes thought. All thought is equal insofar as it "determined-in-the-last-instance" by the Real.

The term "determination-in-the-last-instance" is another constant motif in Laruelle. It is so often repeated that Laruelle often shortens it to "DLI." The term (which bears a trace of Althusser's Marxism) serves as a placeholder in Laruelle's corpus: it signifies his conviction that while the Real is not knowable in itself, the Real is determinant of every instance and every thought immanent to it. It is Laruelle's minimal theory of causation. The Real is causal in the last instance but there is no way to trace this "last instance" back to its source—the Real—for the Real cannot be grasped in terms of what it is. The Real is thus decisive or determinant "in-the-last-instance" of any thought (philosophical or not).

Laruelle sees all philosophies and non-standard philosophies (for there is not one) as immanent to the Real. All thought is immanently a part of the Real. Thought does not operate at some distance from the Real. It is part of the Real and conditioned by it as is all phenomena. The traditional disputes of standard philosophy largely stem from the fact that each perceives itself as solely sufficient to capture the Real. But seen from a non-philosophical perspective, standard philosophies are leveled out. Each is part of the immanence of the Real and each is conditioned by it. This does not mean that non-philosophy takes a wholly relativist view of standard philosophies. Philosophies can be more or less sensible, more or less systematic, more or less ethical, but they are "equal" in the sense that none is ultimately sufficient to capture the Real. Non-philosophy envisions the competing claims of standard philosophy as simply different "materials," which all limited and insufficient to frame, capture, or authoritatively decide the Real. Laruelle's "vision-in-One" is a vision of democratic thought that sees valuable materials for thought in the annals of standard philosophy and in non-philosophical practices, including art.

Laruelle's "naïve" practice of thought is of a cultivated sort. Having, truly and metaphorically, tried to get clear of philosophy, Laruelle opened his work up to a naïve sense of the possible. He opened his thought to the aesthetic and intellectual joy that one can feel on first encountering art or philosophy. Laruelle's non-philosophy holds onto that moment of naïve wonder with philosophy and art before one "learns" the difference between art and philosophy and "learns" the differences between competing schools of thought. Laruelle's ideal reader is, thus, like a lover of fiction or films. Such a lover is not troubled by the different perspectives taken in novels or films.

How we learn philosophy is typically not the way we learn art. We are taught to read philosophical texts as arguments and these arguments are weighted against reality. We come to believe that philosophical schools are incompatible because they make incompatible claims about reality. But if we read philosophy as Laruelle does (and as Rorty wants us to), then we will read it as written raw materials and entirely bracket out what they say concerning the Real. If this seems like a demotion of philosophy (as it does to some of Laruelle's critics), then we might ask: What is it about reading philosophy as "a kind of writing" that demotes philosophy? While, for example, it is standard practice to speak of a "philosophy of literature" or a "philosophy of art," it is non-standard to speak of an "art of philosophy" or a "literature of philosophy." And this is precisely what Laruelle's aesthetic practice of non-philosophy strives for. By bracketing out the question of the Real, Laruelle repurposes the materials of philosophy in new, non-standard, and non-authoritative ways. Non-philosophy is firstly a critique of the authority and power of philosophy and an affirmation of the thoughtfulness, criticality, and creativity of other forms of intellectual expression that do not bear philosophy's authority and approval. Non-aesthetics is not a philosophy of art, but a thinking *according to* art.

Non-philosophy is suspicious of overly professionalized philosophy. It is suspicious of thought that is not a little naïve. A non-philosophical reader is not "only a naïve reader," writes Robin Mackay, "but perhaps also one perturbed by a creeping sense of circumspection of being compelled and interpellated by systems that serve some other authority."[16] Mackay zeroes in on non-philosophy's ethical critique of standard philosophy's authority and the power of the philosophical unconscious. This critique of philosophical authority might seem like a narrowly academic concern. But if we think of standard philosophy in the wider sense as established norms of thinking, then we are in fact dealing also with all those spontaneous philosophies of being and dwelling that go under the names of "individualism," "capitalism," "colonialism," "racism," "hetero-reproductive-sexuality," and so forth. These forms of oppression are also *forms of thought* that have been legitimized and authorized by (and as) forms of power.

Non-philosophy resists being the "subject" of thought and being subjected to its power. Readers of Foucault will no doubt be thinking: this is impossible. We are, according to Foucault, subjects of the forced equation knowledge=power. We are "disciplined" by forms of knowledge and the power they have. How is non-philosophy to respond to Foucault's discourse? In Laruellean fashion, let us take some material from elsewhere: Jean Baudrillard. In *Forget Foucault*, he astutely pointed out that "Foucault's discourse is a mirror of the power it describes."[17] In describing and historicizing power in such minute detail from the macro to the micro level, Foucault's discourse mirrors pervasive, englobing, sovereign implacable power itself. Baudrillard identifies the power of Foucault's discourse as the theoretical mirror image of the very power he critiques. Foucault's critical project is trapped, Baudrillard argues, in a vicious auto-affirming circuit of power discourse. Nothing appears to escape Foucault's project from private intimacies to public executions and this very will-to-know is the mirror image of panoptical power itself. Baudrillard sees Foucault's critical project as fatally fastened on the Real of power such that it can only re-present that power in the mirror of critique. The inevitable effect of this is to reproduce the very reality-effects of power in theory itself. Baudrillard, by contrast, seeks a path beyond critique or a theory no longer invested in unmasking the Real. As he notes in an interview with Sylvere Lotringer:

> What is analysis? As long as you consider that there is a real world, then by the same token there is a possible position for theory. Let us say a dialectical position for the sake of argument. Theory and reality can still be exchanged at some point—and that is ideality. There is after all a point of contact between the two. And then you can transform the world, and theory does transform the world. That is not at all my position anymore. Moreover, it never was.[18]

Baudrillard rejects the representationalist metaphysics of standard philosophical criticism. For him, like for Laruelle, standard philosophical criticism's "reflection" of the Real is in fact its self-projected image of the world. The "mirror" of philosophical criticism is in actuality a projection screen. Theory and criticism for Baudrillard must jettison the representationalist metaphysics of reflection in the name of "challenging the real."[19] Challenge here means a duel with reality or its parallel. "At that point, theory is no longer theory," notes Baudrillard, "it is the event itself."[20] Theory ceases to be theory in the standard sense once it gives up the principle of reality or the Real. It becomes then what Baudrillard calls "theory-fiction"—a parallel discourse to the standard critical discourse on the Real. On this point, Laruelle is close to Baudrillard's non-standard conception of theory. Like Baudrillard, Laruelle axiomatically rejects the standard concept of theory as mirror of the Real. And he too operationalizes the term "fiction" to denote his non-standard practice of theory (or philosophy). But Laruelle's fictional challenge to standard philosophy has an ethical charge not found in Baudrillard's theory-fictions. Laruelle's fictions aim to think the human without victimizing the human by means of philosophical abstraction.

Human and victim

Laruelle belongs to the same generation that gave us so many luminaries of "French Theory": Jacques Derrida, Luce Irigaray, Jean Baudrillard, Hélène Cixous, Gilles Deleuze, Michel Foucault, Louis Althusser, and many others. He shares with the "poststructuralist" generation a commitment to immanent and anti-foundationalist thought. But Laruelle differs from poststructuralist thinkers in one radical respect. He unabashedly affirms the human and humanity. He has refused to adopt a stance of anti-humanism, posthumanism, and various other attempts to decenter "the human" or "the subject" of the "human sciences" or the "humanities."

The poststructural project of decentering and deconstructing human-centric thought in the name of minoritarian and marginalized bodies and ways of being is not in itself rejected by Laruelle. He is not a reactionary who would like to see the privileged, white, which

Laruelle male, body re-installed as the center and symbol of "man,"
"humanism," and "humanity." Rather, both schools of thought—
the old humanism and posthumanism—are seen from Laruelle's
perspective of "vision-in-One" as equally determined by a decision
on what the human is. Both schools subject the human to a discourse
of power. Laruelle looks for something less "human" in the humanist
sense and more "humane" in the basic and generic sense. He will
call this naïve figure of the generically human by a variety of names:
"human-in-human," "man-in-person," or simply "human." The names
are multiple but the idea is singular: the "human" figures life lived in
the Real. What more does he say? Not much. To say too much, to
specify too much, what this generic human is would lend itself to
a discourse determined in the last instance by some final decision
regarding what the human is. The human in Laruelle's discourse is
a figure for the Real of human life that cannot (and should not) be
reduced to a discourse of knowledge/power.

Laruelle places and prioritizes the human in its generic and lived
reality before all else. The human is positioned in his discourse as
prior to any decision on the Real that philosophy might take and it
is prior to any philosophical projection of the Real—what Laruelle
calls the "World." The figure of the generically human resonates in
Laruelle's recollection of his departure for non-philosophy. Having
"cleared away all the books," Laruelle notes, "I started again with a
new blank sheet of paper, and I began to search myself."[21] Laruelle's
journey toward non-philosophy was not a simple wiping away of his
philosophical training. It was not merely a case of wiping the slate
clean—a tabula rasa. It was a "new" blank sheet of paper, a "new"
thought. Isolated and without mooring in ready-to-hand philosophy
books, Laruelle found himself alone and searching himself. The
figure of a human without philosophy immersed in the immanence
of the non-philosophizable Real of lived life; this figure of the young
Laruelle is the autobiographical figuration of the human of his non-
philosophical project. The human without definition—the human
beyond definition—as an existent, concrete, lived reality is the living
allegory of non-philosophy.

The human of the everyday life-world rarely makes an appearance
in philosophy with the exception of certain strains of phenomenology
from Husserl, to Heidegger, through to Merleau-Ponty and Fanon.

Each of these thinkers in very different ways looked for the unremarked and unremarkable in life. They start with the simple and banal experiences of the everyday from a walk in the Black Forest (Heidegger) to a walk in racist Paris (Fanon). Laruelle retains the phenomenological tradition's prizing of everyday experience. He retains phenomenology's "naïve" commitment to thinking everyday human experience. But the question for Laruelle is: How can we think the human without *philosophizing humanity* and thereby transfiguring human experience into a "subject" of philosophical reflection or projection? Laruelle writes that non-philosophy is "centered on the term man," or human, but this centering of the term is not taken to be a definitional, restrictive, or philosophical centering of "the human" as "subject."[22]

The human for Laruelle is "not really a center, since 'man' is a somewhat marginal instance of a theoretical apparatus that is necessary to approach the problem of man."[23] In other words, "man" is precisely an *abstraction* in Laruelle's theoretical apparatus of non-philosophy, but one that is necessary to merely mark a point from which to "approach the problem of man." The human of lived life is thus precisely not the "man" of non-philosophy. The "man" of non-philosophy marks an abstraction that non-philosophy seeks to displace in its attempt to think the human as irreducible to any philosophical or theoretical abstraction. Laruelle freely admits that the insistence on the abstraction of "man" as a means of challenging standard philosophical abstractionism is a "paradox."[24] Laruelle continues:

> This is a difficult thought for those who are not initiated in philosophy. Although for philosophers themselves it is also very difficult, because it goes counter to philosophy as traditionally practiced. . . . But at the same time it is a thought that claimed from the start to be for the ordinary man. So, the paradox of non-standard thought is that it struggles against philosophy, against philosophical authority, and it does so by making use of philosophy (and of science also—the combination of the two is very important); but at the same time, it is undertaken so as to avail oneself of a field of experience (itself rather paradoxical) that might be called the human phenomenon or phenomena.[25]

Non-philosophy's thought in general, and of the human in particular, again, does not negate philosophy. Rather it "uses" philosophy and "science" (about which we will hear more) against philosophy and its "authority." Here one can detect a certain deconstructive way of thinking; the use of philosophy against its supposed authority is crucial to the work of Derrida, Paul de Man, and many others of the school of deconstruction. Where non-philosophy differs from deconstruction, however, is in its *constructive* project to think beyond the bounds of critique.

The "man" of non-philosophy is a figure radically distinct from what Laruelle calls the "World." The World at issue for Laruelle is a philosophical abstraction—a *worldview*—which philosophy frames as a "reflection" of the Real, but which Laruelle sees as the *projected* image of the Real within philosophy. The human, for Laruelle, is therefore beyond and before the philosophical projection of the World. "The humanity of generic man," writes Laruelle "is radically distinct from the world—which is not to say absolutely distinct."[26] There is no way entirely to distinguish the human from a certain conscious or unconscious philosophical conception of the world of humanity. Even an entirely negative definition of the human—the human as philosophically indefinable—is still to an extent a philosophical abstraction.

Philosophy typically defines the human in relation to its conception of the world. Hobbes, for example, conceptualized the human on the basis of his anthropology of society. Humans are free in the state of nature—a world without organized polities and hierarchized political structures—but they willingly give up this freedom and promise obedience to an organized state in exchange for security and protection. Thus, Hobbes's concept of the human is a being motivated by fear of the world. The world, conceived as a threatening place of insecurity and ruthless competition, is the backdrop against which Hobbes fashions his model of the human. Or, in Marx, for another example, we find that he begins with a certain conception of the world, a world of materialist striving, class conflict, and capitalist exploitation, from which he derives the figure of the alienated human "producer" who is doubly figured as an exploited subject and as the revolutionary subject of history

Laruelle's thought of the human is, again, in a sense knowingly naïve. He insists that the human be countenanced in thought without reducing the human to a *subject of thought*. Laruelle de-defines and de-philosophizes "the human" so as not to reproduce the violence of abstraction that victimizes the human in the Real. This is Laruelle's most ethically damning charge of philosophy. Standard philosophy, when it thinks the human, engages in a violent and victimizing gesture. The human ceases to be human and becomes the "subject" of a knowledge/power discourse. This problem of victimization is redoubled and rendered still more problematic by philosophy's attempt to think the victim.

While standard philosophy's tendency is to abstract the human, the victim barely registers on its radar. Cornell West powerfully and persuasively insists that an ethical conception of the human ought to begin with the Latin etymological root "humando"—something that must be buried.[27] We must begin with a recognition of the concrete life and death of the human. West's image of the human is rooted in the image of the corpse, in the body, and bodies of death and catastrophe. Human catastrophe and human-made catastrophes— from slavery to the Shoah, to the ongoing *al-Nakba* (catastrophe) of Palestinian life—is the ethical backdrop for thinking the human. Heidegger, for example, argued in *Being and Time* that that "being concerned with being"—*Dasein*—is a "being-toward-death." But death remains for Heidegger an abstraction on the horizon, a subject of thought, but not experience.

West, and all those who begin with catastrophe and corpses such as Cornell West, Edward Said, Primo Levi, Malcolm X, and so many others, ethically require that we begin with a concrete conception of the human as a suffering, dying, and dead body. Such thought does not begin with the exalted human body on the Grecian pedestal, but with the body in the mass grave—the victim. Thinking in this way means confronting the ugliness of victimization and to close what Laruelle terms "victimological distance." In a collection of interviews with Philippe Petit, Laruelle responds to the question of the work of philosophical distance with respect to the victim.

It is not a simple distance, able to be measured empirically or geometrically. It has a doubled dimension, two kinds of ekstasis and not a single one. The first kind of distance belongs to what I would call the "laid-out Victim," but laid flat next to the nudity of history, on the ground of time and space, and this is not a metaphor, this is the Victim given horizontally, under her most intuitive form. And then there is another dimension of the Victim, this is the Victim that I will call the "standing" or vertical Victim—so, for example, the crucified Victim—this is Christ as the exemplary victim, abased but still standing.[28]

Laruelle is here working out the concept of the Victim by using the "raw materials" furnished to him by imagery and philosophy. The "horizontal victim" is the dimension of the dead—the corpse. It is the dimension emblematized in the searing images of the killing fields: mass graves, piled corpses, undignified death, banalized murder. The "vertical victim" is the victim beaten, but yet not dead. We see the verticality of victimization in the crucifix, but also in so many other images. It is the victim still standing, for example, in Picasso's *Guernica* of 1937. The image confronts us with the destroyed, terrorized victims of the Nazi's cynical and heartless bombing of the small and defenseless town of Guernica done as a favor to General Franco whose fascist forces were at that moment fully engaged in a militarized effort to annihilate Spain's democratic forces. Picasso shows Guernica wounded but still standing. It is a cry not only for Spain, but a cry to the world to see, recognize, and respond to the catastrophic. The standing bull in the corner contrasts with the figures of horizontal victimization: a dead soldier on the ground and a lifeless child suspended in her mother's arms.

Even closer to Laruelle's theory of the vertical victim is the emaciated figures of Alberto Giacometti (Figure 2). The figures in *City Square* (1948), for example, stand stiffly, isolated, psychologically distant from one another, haunting an absent (or destroyed) town square: ghostly indices of the catastrophe of the Second World War. Picasso, Giacometti, and the countless anonymous painters of the crucifixion give us the image of the vertical victim. The vertical victim is always attached to a moment of decision and choice. How are we to face and respond to the victim and the catastrophe for which the victim stands? The impassioned effort by artists like Picasso and Giacometti is to represent the victim without distancing the victim from the viewer. The vertical victim confronts us head-on. We are implored to respond to what is still living and is, therefore, a matter of

FIGURE 2 *Alberto Giacometti,* City Square, *1948.*

Source: Giacometti, Alberto (1901–66) © VAGA & ARS, NY City Square, 1948. Bronze, 21.6 × 64.5 × 43.8 cm Purchase. Museum of Modern Art, Digital Image ©The Museum of Modern Art/Licensed by SCALA/Art Resource, NY © 2018 Alberto Giacometti Estate/VAGA at Artists Rights Society (ARS), NY.

futurity and justice for the past. The anonymous and deterritorialized victims seen in *City Square* or *Guernica* make material and palpable the reality of isolation, desolation, and silence that haunts the aftermath of catastrophe and historical trauma. But it also makes an ethical claim on us in the here and now. It asks us to respond justly to injustice on the basis of what is concrete and real in all that is human in an inhuman world.

The victim without world, without justice, without explanation, or philosophical justification is the point of departure for Laruelle's ethics. The ethical dimension of non-philosophy is signified by the victim, but an ethics of thought is integral to its logic from the first to the last. Laruelle's critique of Philosophical Decision, and his insistence on the insufficiency of philosophy to think the Real, holds an ethical charge for it resists affirming and reifying the authority of philosophy. The ethics of non-philosophy resists philosophical authority (and authoritarianism) in the name of the Real and its concrete victims as well as all those "subjects" victimized by philosophical abstraction.

Now, it is important to point out that Laruelle's critique of the philosophical abstraction of victims—a charge he has leveled, for example, at Alain Badiou who continues to affirm a Maoist line even at the expense of Mao's victims—is, however, not restricted to the work of standard philosophy. Laruelle sees Philosophical Decision at work in fields far removed from the academic practice of philosophy. It exists (or is enacted) anywhere that the work of decision and abstraction functionally decide the Real, and via this decision, produce an authoritative image of the World. Laruelle therefore sees the media as "philosophical" for it decides on the Real by determining which realities are really important, and thereby projects a mediatized image of the real or really important "World." Laruelle writes:

> In a general way, within an ontological representation of the Victim, she is only originally present with some distance, a distance I call *victimological distance*. Even when she seems given in some very immediate way as in the case of television images, the Victim is, in reality, given across a distance, that of the image. This distance is the mark of philosophy.[29]

It is no accident that terms like "World," "Globe," or "Times" circulate with such frequency in the titles of newspapers, magazines, and television news. Media outlets trade on their authority to decide and image the world and the times we live in. It is in their authoritative decisiveness with respect to imaging the world that Laruelle detects the unmistakable trace of philosophy. But, how does this victimization via standard philosophy operate in the sphere of art and aesthetics?

Victimizing art

While the human victim is the central ethical figure of Laruelle's work, the theme of philosophical victimization is important to his work on art. Laruelle resists the philosophical temptation to dominate art through the practice of philosophical or theoretical aesthetics.

The ancient Greeks held that "beauty" was inseparable from art. And since Kant, philosophical aesthetics has been concerned with judging what is beautiful or not. But since the advent of modernist art, we no longer assume that art and beauty go together in every instance. And certainly, since the advent of Marcel Duchamp's "readymade" art—such as a urinal, bottle rack, typewriter case, or bicycle wheel—the philosophical question of art has been dissociable from the question of beauty. Today, aesthetics also deals with fundamental questions concerning the ontology of art and the sociology of taste. The result is that the domain of philosophical aesthetics has expanded to a vast extent. It covers everything from a coatrack by Duchamp, to home furnishings, fashion, as well as architecture, photography, literature, and their various intersectional crossing into sociology, politics, history, and cultural studies. This expansion of "the aesthetic," as a field of inquiry, has also expanded the authority of philosophy. It is this authority of philosophy, and its domination over the meaning of art, that Laruelle calls into question.

The domination of art by aesthetics victimizes art by negating its immanent philosophical content. Laruelle holds to the idea that art is itself always already immanently theoretical or philosophical. This idea is itself not especially new. One can find a similar line of thought in the work of Adorno, Benjamin, and Derrida (among many others) who in different ways were keen to point out that any theory of art must first take into account the theoretical content of art itself. Laruelle shares with such thinkers the conviction that theoretical content exists within the immanent structure and signifying force of the work of art. But where he takes his distance from this school of thought is in his refusal to "explicate" or "interpret" that content. It is precisely in the explicative gesture of philosophical aesthetics that Philosophical Decision is performed and the authority vested in the work of art is transferred to the philosophical explicator or judge. This auto-transference of authority ultimately reaffirms the oldest of philosophical prejudices—a prejudice inaugurated by Plato—that art is to be explained and judged by the authority vested in philosophy.

To put this into more concrete terms, as I write this, I am listening to John Coltrane's *A Love Supreme* from 1964 on YouTube. One of the commenters wrote, "I love hip-hop, but this shit is touching me somewhere down inside, I don't know how to describe [it,] it doesn't make me want to get up and dance but it makes me think what have I done with my life, hmm. Strange."[30] Art can make us think deeply because it is, at least in the work of artists like Coltrane, already a deep thought even if that thought is difficult or even impossible to translate. The materiality of art—sound, color, textuality, space, and so forth—is taken by standard aesthetics as a material to be worked and shaped into meaning and interpretive significance. The materiality of art is transcoded and *overcoded* by philosophical practice. Laruelle's non-philosophical approach to art, by contrast, is to use the *materiality of philosophy* to make an *art of philosophy*. Laruelle notes:

> My problem is really that of how to treat philosophy as a material, and thus also as a materiality—without preoccupying oneself with the aims of philosophy, of its dignity, of its quasi-theological ends, of philosophical virtues, wisdom. . . . None of that interests me. What interests me is philosophy as the material for an art, at the limit, an art. My idea . . . is to make art with philosophy, to introduce or make a poetry of thought, not necessarily a poetry made of concepts, a poetry that would put forward some philosophical thesis—but to make something poetic with concepts. Thus, to create a practice that could destroy, in a certain way, the classical usage of philosophy.[31]

Laruelle seeks an art of philosophy rather than a philosophy of art. The late Heidegger had tried something similar, but Laruelle takes a step beyond Heidegger's approach in, again, refusing the philosophic temptation to decide on the meaning of a work of art and judge its aesthetic success. Instead, Laruelle wants to create a *parallel practice* to art in the field of non-philosophy. The aim is not to interpret art and create via interpretation a critical mimesis of the work of art, but rather to take artmaking as a model for doing philosophy. Again, this is not without precedent. Derrida's experimental texts, as we noted, bear similarity to Laruelle's approach. But Derrida's daring is somewhat tempered by Derrida's philosophical program. Whatever one might think on first reading these texts by Derrida is apt to be refined and grounded by interpreting them in light of his larger and fairly systematic philosophical program. It is precisely this grounding in (and by) philosophy that Laruelle's experimental approach to aesthetics foregoes. In this, his *art of philosophy* bears comparison to Marcel Duchamp's *philosophy of art*. A detour through Duchamp, and the problem of reading his work represents, provides a useful parallel for thinking through the problem of how to read Laruelle non-philosophically.

The problem of reading Duchamp

Duchamp was certainly one of the most "philosophical" artists of the twentieth century. His so-called readymade artworks—most memorably his *Fountain* of 1917—called into question the standard assumptions that had until that moment grounded the practice and theory of art (Figure 3). *Fountain* is found and not made; it exhibits little to no aesthetic content; it is commercial, industrial, everyday—banal. Lionized by the artists of the 1960s, notably Andy Warhol, Robert Rauschenberg, and Conceptual artists such as Joseph Kosuth, Duchamp was, however, largely marginalized in the first historical accountings of modern art. His work, which questions the standard concept of the artwork itself, had no apparent parallel in the work of modernist artists from Matisse and Picasso to Mondrian and Pollock.

The modernist movements from French Realism through Cubism to Abstract Expressionism were understood by formalist critics, such as Clement Greenberg, as a series of "self-critical" attempts to uncover a purified ontology of painting and sculpture. But Duchamp's work did not fit the formalist frame, for his work precisely challenged the value of formal innovation itself. His subsequent embrace by artists of the 1960s has retrospectively posited Duchamp as the "father of postmodernism." His readymade art is reflected in the consumer products of Pop, in the object-oriented impulse of Minimalism, and in the "anti-retinal" art of Conceptualism.

The problem with this historical schema, still quite popular in art history classes, is that art-historical modernism (1840–1960) and art-historical postmodernism (1960–present?) reifies precisely the kind of linear, encompassing narrative that postmodern thought calls into question. It was, Jean-François Lyotard, after all, who, in *The Postmodern Condition*, argued that postmodernity is precisely marked by a creeping suspicion or "incredulity" with respect to "grand narratives" of historical progression whether in art, politics, or culture generally.[32] Standard art-historical accounts structure the modernism/postmodernism divide through "a periodizing and idealist logic," writes Amelia Jones, that is "thoroughly characteristic of the modern."[33] Jones takes her cue from Lyotard and from Craig Owens in her attempt to rethink the legacy of Duchamp's art without reifying the linear logic of modernist art historiography. "The postmodernism

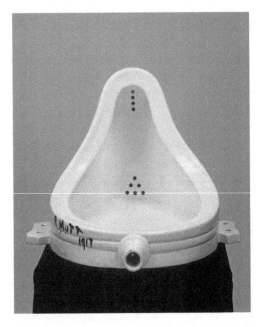

FIGURE 3 *Marcel Duchamp*, Fountain, *1917 (replica 1964).*

Source: Duchamp, Marcel (1887–1968) © ARS, NY. Fountain. 1917/1964. Third version, replicated under the direction of the artist in 1964 by the Galarie Shwartz, Milan. Glazed ceramic, 63 × 48 × 35 cm. AMI 1986-295. Photo: Philippe Migeat/ Christian Bahier. Musee National d'Art Moderne © CNAC/MNAM/Dist. RMN-Grand Palais/Art Resource, NY © Association Marcel Duchamp/ADAGP, Paris/ Artists Rights Society (ARS), New York 2018.

I am concerned with," writes Jones, "is that articulation of what art critic Craig Owens has called a 'counter-discourse' to a rather narrowly defined modernism, which it poses itself as superseding: This postmodernism stages itself as the negation of modernism, as its radical *other.*"[34] Yet, Jones is not entirely satisfied with this schema either because it is too easily reified into precisely the *other of modernism* whose identity is retroactively stabilized in contrast to the challenge of postmodernism. The point for Jones is to ask: How does Duchamp's "postmodern" art challenge our assumptions concerning the stability of the category "modernism"? What version of modernism does Duchamp challenge? Jones's answer is that the modernism at issue for Duchamp is precisely that "modernism" enshrined in the practice of modern art historiography.

Duchamp challenged the modern foundations of the discipline of art history itself. The modern practice of art history was formalized in the early twentieth century by historians who took the aesthetics of art and the life of the artist as the twin pillars of art historiographic practice. Jones writes:

> Art history, in its academic and museological, institutional and discursive forms, still writes its history via the individual artist, and it is the divinity of the artist that secures both the identity of the interpreter and the literal economic value of the object of art.[35]

Art history has a vested interest in maintaining its modern paradigm because the value of art is tied to what might be called the "authentication business" transacted by art historians and museum professionals, which ultimately serves the needs of the art market. Jones's thesis is perhaps best supported by the ironic museological territorialization of Duchamp's work since the 1960s. *Fountain*, along with Duchamp's other readymades, is today an icon of twentieth-century art, gracing the cover of art history textbooks and only half ironically protected in a glass vitrine at the Philadelphia Museum of Modern Art where it sits on permanent display. Duchamp's effort to trouble the modernist prejudice for the original, authentic, and handmade with a readymade piece of industrial plumbing, signed with a pseudonym (R. Mutt), is now a cornerstone of his oeuvre and is the lynchpin of postmodern art history. This domestication of Duchamp is testament to the influence that the tradition of connoisseurship continues to exert over the practice and teaching of art history.

One of the principal reasons why Duchamp's readymades were largely ignored by modern art historians was because they did not judge them to be aesthetic objects, and for that reason, not works of art. Ironically, today the claim is often made, by self-proclaimed postmodern art historians, that Duchamp was an *original* artist because his idea that an artwork does not have to be aesthetically pleasing was an *original contribution to art history*! As Dalia Judovitz observes:

> The ready-made is the culmination of Duchamp's critique of artistic vision, a critique seeking to transform that vision, to undermine its optical verisimilitude by reinscribing it through verbal and

cognitive activity. . . . This invocation of "visual indifference" marks Duchamp's turn away from the "visual" arts toward an art that seeks to define itself in terms of its intellectual rather than "retinal" potential.[36]

Judovitz's suggestion here, incisive and precise, is, however, marked by the trace of modern art historiography identified by Jones. This trace is evident in Judovitz's centralization of Duchamp's critical *vision*, which is figured as a challenge to the norm of "artistic vision." But still, it is the artist's "vision" that is made, once again, the art-historical marker of significance: the singular vision of the artist—the genius. Duchamp's "turn" from an "artistic" to a "critical vision" is figured as a turning point in art history thereby securing once again the standard art-historical suturing of the historical to the personal, and the transubjective to the subjectivity of vision. The subject of vision and the vision of art history are collapsed by Judovitz into a symmetrical manifold of facticity.

The enigma of Duchamp: How to think his challenge to modernism without reinscribing that challenge within the value-laded frame of modernism? How do we recognize the critique of originality, the deconstruction of authorship and the expressive, psycho-biographical self without reifying that critique into a historiographical projection that would simply reaffirm the centrality of the visionary artist as the historically determinant force in the movement of art history? How can we be truly postmodern? Or, put differently: How can we be non-modern?

The problem of reading Laruelle

The problem of how to read Duchamp's "postmodernist" art without recourse to modernist art-historiographic frameworks parallels the problem of how to read Laruelle's non-philosophical work without recourse to standard philosophical frameworks. For to read non-philosophy as simply a "critique" of philosophy immediately collapses it back into standard philosophy, which since Kant, has been a critical practice. Another parallel: the immanent values inscribed within the practice of art history in its modern form is found in the standard approach to the history of philosophy. The centrality of the artist in art history parallels the centrality of the philosopher in philosophy. Both disciplines have a tendency to collapse "history" into the privileged "vision" of a subject of creative or critical thought. The ease with which both disciplines use the name of the artist or thinker interchangeably with his or her work, for example, "Platonic," "Derridean," "Duchampian," or, for that matter "Laruellean" is the sign and symptom of a forcing of the equation: subject=history. Jones's problematic of how to read Duchamp's "postmodern" work without reaffirming the centrality of the visionary artist—long the cornerstone of modern art historiography—parallels the principal methodological question for readers of non-philosophy: How to read non-philosophy non-philosophically?

As noted at the beginning of this chapter, John O' Maoilearca argues that the problem of how to read Laruelle non-philosophically is a crucial methodological and theoretical question that cannot be ignored if non-philosophy is to be taken seriously. Just as Jones struggles to read Duchamp in a truly "postmodern" way that will not reaffirm the values of modern art historiography, so O' Maoilearca sets himself the challenge to read (and explicate) Laruelle non-philosophically. The first move that he makes is to seize on the ethical dimension of non-philosophy. Recall that non-philosophy rejects the Principle of Sufficient Philosophy. Since no philosophy is sufficient to think the immanence of the Real, then neither is any philosophy more right or wrong *in this regard*. This does not mean, as some critics charge, that non-philosophy is nihilistic or simply relativistic. It is not that all thought is equal in *all ways*. Not at all: *non-philosophy sees all standard philosophies as equal only insofar as they are all insufficient with respect to the Real, but they are insufficient in this regard in different ways*. Non-philosophy conceives of the "ideas of philosophy," writes O' Maoilearca, as "no longer positions to be argued with, critiqued, accepted, or promoted but raw material to be utilized."[37] Of course, this begs the question: Utilized for what? "The function of non-philosophy," O' Maoilearca concludes, "is to integrate (rather than reduce, replace, or eliminate) philosophical views back into the Real by surveying them together in a democratic, immanent, revision where no view is superior to any other."[38]

Laruelle's method is to resituate philosophy as part of the Real—as not decisive of, but decided by, the Real. Laruelle's work is an attempt to bring about a "real integration" of philosophy back into the Real.[39] Laruelle's perspective of "vision-in-One" looks not upon the Real, but at the insufficiency of philosophy to grasp it. Laruelle writes:

> Non-philosophy has two aspects: on the one hand, it reduces philosophy to a state of whatever material; on the other hand, it announces new positive rules (which are non-philosophical but deduced from vision-in-One) of the labor of this material. By presenting these rules without yet founding them, we are giving a very succinct and elementary idea of their founding, which is vision-in-One.[40]

The "positive rules" of non-philosophy are rules of freedom: it is the freedom to combine, collate, mix, and hybridize philosophies. Vision-in-One leads to "new" rules to philosophize philosophy as raw material. The "heresy" of non-philosophy lies in its sheer agnosticism with respect to the final truths of philosophy. Vision-in-One opens an alternate way of seeing philosophy. Laruelle writes:

> Philosophy is not just a set of categories and objects, syntaxes and experiences or operations of decision and position: it is animated and traversed by faith or belief in itself as in absolute reality, by an intentionality or reference to the real which it claims to describe and even constitute. . . . This is its fundamental auto-position, which can also be called auto-factualization, or auto-festishization—all of which we label as the Principle of Sufficient Philosophy. The suspension of these phenomena [in non-philosophy] amounts to a defactualization, defetishization, or deposition of philosophical decision, to its reduction to the state of a material.[41]

Rocco Gangle, in his incisive reading of Laruelle's *Philosophies of Difference* concisely captures the non-philosophical stakes of "vision-in-One:"

> How does Vision-in-One respond to the traditional, indeed constituting question of ideality and reality? Rather than providing

a new and different answer to this perennial question, non-philosophy . . . provides a new strategy for understanding it *as a problem*. This strategy consists of placing oneself, as a thinker, within a stance that sees the problem as simply an effect of using [philosophical] thought. . . . That is, it notes the problem as merely an instance of philosophy.[42]

Gangle importantly (and correctly) identifies the "stance" of non-philosophy as a stance of recognition of, and resistance to, the structural effects of standard philosophical discourses. His emphasis on non-philosophy as a "strategy" also importantly highlights the interventionist streak in non-philosophical practice. Non-philosophy is strategic doing, a strategic use of style and syntax, aimed at the maintenance of a stance of radical indifference with respect to the decisionist temptations and authoritarian effects of standard philosophy.

The power of philosophy enshrined in what Laruelle calls its Principle of Sufficient Philosophy is dethroned or defetishized from the radical perspective of "vision-in-One." To see philosophy as raw material is to see it no longer as an exalted set of grand finalities, but as raw material that may take potentially any shape whatsoever. Laruelle hints at this when he writes that a defetishized vision of philosophy as raw material is induced by treating philosophy as "*whatever material or as whatever given*."[43] This "whatever" appears to operate in two senses: philosophy may become "whatever" in the sense that it can be made from "whatever material," and in the sense that philosophy ought to be treated with a note of indifference, with a "whatever" attitude. The sanctity and authority of philosophy is divested in the gesture of non-philosophy. It is "a question of suspending or bracketing, from vision-in-One, philosophy's legislation, its teleology that makes it the goal of itself: a question of lifting philosophy's circularity or what must still be called its auto-position as absolute fact, tradition or unavoidable 'destiny.'"[44] Non-philosophy is first then a strategic suspension of the auto-legislating and auto-legitimating function of standard philosophy. It derails it from auto-fulfilling its self-projected teleology and destiny. It de-authorizes philosophy.

The insight of Laruelle notwithstanding, one must acknowledge a constitutive blindness in his elaboration of non-philosophy. The central non-philosophical method—reduction of standard philosophy to "raw materials," and these materials rendered as equally insufficient—at once defetishizes philosophical authority, but at the same this method grants non-philosophy the *authority to operationalize this very defetishization*. Indeed, the elaboration of what non-philosophy is—a question whose answer is modified over numerous texts—is a central motif of his work. There is then, one might argue, a *festishization of the very term "non-philosophy,"* which commentators such as O' Maoilearca recognize as problematic. The status of this question is what Laruelle would call "amphibological": the problematic status of the definition of non-philosophy is that it is constitutively unclear if the question—what is non-philosophy?—is itself a philosophical or non-philosophical question. There is no clear way (or method) to read non-philosophy non-philosophically for it cannot be decided if the very question of non-philosophy's identity is a philosophical or non-philosophical question.

An ontology of non-philosophy?

Readers and scholars of Laruelle face a complex question: What is non-philosophy? Does posing this very question not inscribe a standard philosophical bias in the very question itself? Laruelle has explicated his basic idea of non-philosophy over the course of many works spanning decades. But each time, the ontology of non-philosophy is deferred. Its parameters are only negatively constrained by Laruelle's axiomatic rejection of Philosophical Decision and the Principle of Sufficient Philosophy. Beyond these axiomatic starting points, Laruelle offers little in the way of positive doctrine. Here Laruelle is close to Derrida's early formulation of "deconstruction," which demurred positing a doctrine (if this was later done by his acolytes is another matter) in favor of an inventive, and often irreverent, dismantling of philosophical frameworks and the authority vested in long-standing and institutionally validated interpretations of the Western philosophical canon.

Derrida and Laruelle were in contact with one another in the early 1970s. Anthony Paul Smith notes that at first "Laruelle was welcomed into the den of deconstructionists."[45] Derrida praised

Laruelle's work as a "powerful elaboration" and there can be little doubt that Derrida's laudatory assessment had in large part to do with the fact that non-philosophy appears to have strong deconstructionist leanings. Derrida, however, ultimately accused Laruelle of repeating a certain "violence . . . of the type you denounce in philosophical society."[46]

One can only wonder what might have happened if Laruelle had not been ultimately rejected by Derrida and his circle. One can imagine that the emergence of the Derrida industry of the 1980s and 1990s would have been very different had Laruelle occupied a position analogous to say that of Jean-Luc Nancy. But it must be said that this turn of events had as much to do with Laruelle as with Derrida. The fact is Laruelle was not a deconstructionist because he was not then (nor now) a follower. He drew then (as now) from the *material* of deconstruction without reifying that material into an authoritative source.

Laruelle's interest in Derrida early on was principally an interest in elaborating a materialist reading of deconstruction. In *Philosophies of Difference*, for example, Laruelle sought to cross-matrix the work of Deleuze and Guattari with that of Derrida. Refusing to choose sides in what is still a rather contentious (if tired) debate between Deleuzians and Derrideans, Laruelle axiomatically levels each discourse by crossing each into that of the other. And he calls out both sides for failing to *think immanence immanently*. Each discourse, argues Laruelle, retains a certain secretive filiation with the logic of transcendence albeit in the language and frameworks of immanence. Laruelle's reading constructs what Deleuze and Guattari would call an "abstract machine" into which he plugs Deleuzian and Derridean concepts in order to produce a new "plane of immanence" of "Delida/Derreauze" intertextual intensities. Laruelle writes:

I have . . . tried to make the series Delida/Derreuze resonate (these "proper" names function as libidinal intensities . . . they interpenetrate each other and impinge one upon the other, disappropriating one by the other, to the great displeasure, we hope, of the epigonal appropriations and hasty oppositions . . .) repeating deconstruction within the signs of intensive productions . . . within textuality, causing intensive difference and textual simulacrum to communicate, within a reciprocal parody that sometimes displaces deconstruction and intensifies it right up to active and affirmative difference.[47]

Laruelle's ingenious move is to neither repeat a Derridean or a Deleuzian gesture. His reading rather tracks through their texts following an intertextual itinerary (which is perhaps closer to the work of Julia Kristeva than Derrida or Deleuze and Guattari). Those who made their careers through "epigonal appropriations" of Derrida and Deleuze will find Laruelle's work hasty and indelicate in its smashing together of these two divergent discourses. But such is the objection made in the name of Philosophical Decision: a belief that Deleuzian and Derridean philosophies are different "philosophies of difference" for they decide and mark the Real in very different ways. Laruelle suspends that question and discovers in true Derridean and Deleuzian fashion a wealth of "writing" (in Derrida's sense) and host of textual "machines" and discursive "flows" (in Deleuze and Guattari's sense). Laruelle's philosophical mash-up produces a "machinic" re-description of deconstructive thought. "Like Deleuze and Guattari in *Anti-Oedipus*," writes Smith, "Laruelle focuses on the ways in which texts are shown to couple with other texts in deconstruction. These texts function like machines that may be plugged into other machines, allowing for flows between them."[48]

Laruelle affirms the best of poststructuralist sensibilities in his refusal to reify the proper names of the philosophical tradition— even the tradition of poststructuralism itself—and as a consequence he has advocated for a radically intertextual approach to doing philosophy that blends the conceptual creativity of Deleuze and Guattari with the deconstructive protocols of Derrida's thought. The result is, however, quite unlike anything by Deleuze and Guattari or by Derrida. Laruelle's texts neither read like deconstructive "close readings" nor do they speed along at the rate of Deleuzian textual machines. He affirms, in Derridean fashion, the critique of presence and transcendence without, however, transcendentalizing deferral, absence, and immanence. This effort is accomplished, however, less by positing concepts (indeed, we will discuss what becomes of the concept in Chapter 2) than by constructing a prose style and syntax of expression aimed at tripping up the machines of transcendence and presence. His philosophy, as he has maintained for some time now, is better described as a "philo-fiction"—a form of philosophic prose that mimes or "clones" the style of creative writing. He is certainly not the first philosopher to do this. As noted, Derrida was no stranger to experimentations with the prose of philosophy. Derrida's most experimental texts such as *Glas*, *The Post Card*, or *Dissemination* experiment with the prose of standard philosophical exposition. Their shock—and they were shocking in the 1970s and 1980s—had everything to do with the fact that they were written by a self-identified "philosopher."

Laruelle's experimental texts are different. They are less concerned to experiment philosophically than they are to position non-philosophy as firstly a creative practice. Laruelle's texts, from the period of non-philosophy onward, do not constitute a theory of writing, literature, or even a theory of the relation between philosophy and writing or literature. Rather, they constitute an effort to put into practice what Derrida had called for in *Of Grammatology*, namely, *the end of the book and the beginning of writing*—a form of thinking understood as generic "writing" without concern for the authority invested in standardized and tightly defined philosophical or literary genres. If philosophy is indeed "a kind of writing" as Rorty (via Derrida) claims, then Laruelle's work is a "kind" of writing that "looks" philosophical but isn't. His writings are composed of "clones" of standard philosophemes. Laruelle's "clones" *look like concepts* but are rendered in a style immanent to non-philosophy. The neologisms and odd turns of phrase characteristic of Laruelle's writing lead the reader ever back into the terrains of non-philosophy. The relentlessly self-referential character of Laruelle's work clones or simulates the immanent condition of thought in the Real. As all thought is immanent to the Real so the clones of non-philosophy are immanent to non-philosophical discourse. The clones of non-philosophy do not purport to make direct "contact" with the Real as do standard philosophical concepts. The non-relation between the clones of non-philosophy and the Real itself clones the non-relationality of the Real to thought itself. The Real encompasses all relations and therefore has only a relation of *non-relation* to all that it encloses including all possible thought.

The immanence of the real

For Laruelle, the ultimate cause of all thought (philosophical or otherwise) is the Real. Philosophy is but one of the "effects of this cause," but the Real itself "does not form a relationship with this cause."[49] Indeed from the "perspective of the cause [the Real], there is no effect."[50] Philosophies of epistemology, politics, ontology, and so forth are "caused" by the Real in the sense that they respond to (and are) effects of the Real. But the Real itself is entirely indifferent to standard philosophy's determinations and decisions on it. And what is true of philosophy proper is true of non-philosophy: for Laruelle both discourses (if that is the right word) are immanently determined by the Real—they are among its "effects," but neither has any effect on the Real. This to be sure strikes one as odd, especially in light of the long history of thought that Andrew Feenberg calls "the philosophy of praxis."[51] The philosophy of praxis (exemplified by the Marxist tradition) is founded on the hope that the Real can be transformed by thought. So, from the perspective of praxis, Laruelle's "unilateral" theory of the Real and its philosophical effects would sound a note of defeatism. But the issue is more complex as any reader of Laruelle's work on Marx soon discovers.

Laruelle refuses to jettison the heritage of praxis philosophy (as, for example, the so-called *nouveaux philosophes* of the 1970s did), but neither is he content to reify and render dogmatic Marx's thought. The point for Laruelle is to recover a philosophy of praxis rooted in the Real. Laruelle's position is not as some might suspect a philosophy of resignation in the face of reality. Rather, it starts from Marx's famed eleventh thesis on Feuerbach: the point is not to interpret the world but to change it. Laruelle radicalizes Marx by seeking out a path of thought that can transcend philosophy itself. Laruelle answers Marx by asserting: *the point is not to philosophize the Real, but to change philosophy in light of the Real.* It is not for Laruelle that the Real is simply an implacable and transcendental finality over which philosophy is powerless. Ideas matter and they can change the world. But they do so only and precisely because they are immanent to its very fabric and, as such, they never have sufficient critical distance or critical clarity to justify knowing and deciding over and upon the Real. Philosophy, far from being a clear-eyed way of deciding on the Real, turns out to be its strangely amphibological double: an inhomogenous mix of critical and creative impulses, insights, logics, metaphors, polemics, and aspirations. This means that the entire approach of non-philosophy strategically (if not systematically) must evade falling into the decisional posture of standard philosophy. It tries never to forget its place as immanent and determined (and "overdetermined") by the matrix of the Real while also never ceasing to struggle to think this very thought as the paradigmatic point of departure for non-philosophy itself.

This stance is also for Laruelle a *style* of practice or even praxis, but of a kind that is immanently constituted through the materiality of forms of writing that Laruelle calls simply "fiction." As we have already noted, this turn to fiction in a certain sense is not unprecedented. Derrida in the 1970s was committed to enacting a practice of philosophical liberation—a liberation from the narrow confines of philosophical tradition—by a generalized "grammatology" that sought to creatively deconstruct the ideological and stylistic borders between literature and philosophy. But he was by no means the only one of his generation to radically rethink and reinvent the norms of philosophical prose. Jean Baudrillard, Luce Irigaray, Hélène Cixous, Gilles Deleuze, Félix Guattari, Roland Barthes, among others, began to think of philosophy as a "kind of writing" in Rorty's sense. The difference with Laruelle is that he does not remain transfixed by the border between philosophy and literature but rather aims to show how that very border is always already inscribed within a certain *philosophical* framing of the problem of "literary" language itself.

The question for Laruelle is not to discover what the relation is between literature and philosophy, but to transcend the very question of the border assumed by that question. His is not a cartographic gesture. It is not a matter of mapping or remapping the landscape of language and its uses. The fixing or deconstructing of genre borders are two sides of the same coin. The problem is how and what to write once this point is axiomatically assumed. The "style it takes," to quote John Cale, is a style of conceptual prose that is neither of the standard philosophical kind nor of a sort that revels in it *not being of that sort* as is the case with much poststructural writing of Laruelle's generation. It must first be a style committed to a "democracy of thought" that is mindful of its relative position within this democratic field of immanent sign-systems. As much by style as by principles and axioms, non-philosophy situates itself within what Laruelle calls the "continent of flat thoughts."[52] This "continent" bears a family-likeness to Deleuze and Guattari's concept of the "plane of immanence"—a conceptual space imagined from the perspective of radical immanence—where differences of thought are imagined as folds in a continuous manifold rather than autonomous and discontinuous spaces. "The One is not transcendent that might contain immanence," writes Deleuze, "but the immanent contained within a transcendental field" and as such "transcendence is always a product of immanence."[53] The only problem that Laruelle has with this conception is that it is a *concept of immanence*. The problem is how to think *immanence immanently* without sneaking transcendence back into the concept of immanence. And, hardest of all, to arrive at an immanent thinking of immanence that understands itself as immanent to the Real in the last instance. How to think a thought about immanence that is immanent to the "continent of flat thought"—the immanent plane of the Real?

Laruelle's term, "continent of flat thoughts" comes not from an engagement with philosophy proper, but from photography. Photography is a form of material thought and practice, a praxis, that envisions a world of visual differences immanently embedded within the continuous and unified manifold of photographic surfaces. The photographic surface for Laruelle is a model for thinking theory in a way that clones the Real abstractly and thus materially underscores its difference from the Real in contrast to representationalist metaphysics. Non-philosophy is no more a reflection of the Real than a photographic image. Both are constructions that parallel rather than reproduce the Real.

Generic science

The style of non-philosophy or its stylistic model is that of science—"generic science." The "science of non-philosophy" is generic in that it takes the open-minded and experimental attitude of the sciences as a general or generic starting point from which to rethink the aims and possibilities of philosophy. One must not be afraid to experiment in science and this courage to experiment is necessary too for non-philosophy. In *Philosophy and Non-Philosophy*, under the heading "A scientific practice of philosophy," Laruelle writes:

> One can obviously be frightened by this radical opening and overwhelmed by vertigo in front of the abyss of apparently "uncontrolled" and uncontrollable possibilities that consequently open with a [scientifically] renewed philosophical practice. At the same time, one can be indecisive facing so many possibilities and perplexed facing the absence of any recognizable standard. But it's not impossible to formulate new rules that permit moving forward in this chaos; for these rules are nothing but those of vision-in-One as science's essence. . . . A science of philosophy . . . means two things immediately for philosophy. First it means philosophy's spontaneous exercise, philosophy's belief-in-itself-as-in-the-real, is a transcendental illusion. . . . The other consequence, which envelops the preceding one, is that, on the basis of a real usage of decision, it becomes possible to radically renew its practices, to *found a real usage of the fictional and hallucinatory virtualities of philosophy—non-philosophy.*[54]

Laruelle clones the experimental impulse of science into the practice of non-philosophy so as to "formulate new rules" regarding the usage of Philosophical Decision. Non-philosophy refuses to reproduce the "spontaneous" belief in philosophy, which collapses into an auto-faith of the Real on which it appears to decide. Non-philosophy instead operationalizes a "real" usage of Philosophical Decision, one which takes as axiomatic that standard philosophy's decision on the Real is always "fictional" and "hallucinatory." Non-philosophy takes this hallucination of the Real produced by Philosophical Decision and radicalizes it to produce a "real" fictional and hallucinatory non-philosophy. Non-philosophy, or "philo-fiction," embraces *the truth of philosophy's fictionalization of the Real* via its decisional dynamic.

Generic science for Laruelle is an immanent cloning of philosophy or put differently: generic science is the proper name for the non-philosophical cloning of standard philosophy. Science is an immanent recasting of philosophy's self-presumed transcendence with respect to the Real. Whereas standard philosophy places itself "outside" the Real by the gesture of Decision, non-philosophy relocates thought within the immanent "continent of flat thoughts." Philosophy is theological inasmuch as it is outside the Real whereas non-philosophy like science adopts a radically immanent perspective. Alexander Galloway captures this point precisely.

> For Laruelle, *philosophy* means roughly "the thing that is *transcendental* vis-à-vis the real." Taken in this sense philosophy is always representational, reflective, or mediated. Philosophy reveals the conditions of possibility of things (but not those things themselves). By contrast, generic science means roughly "the thing that is *immanent* vis-à-vis the real." Science is always direct or radical, not reflective or mediated. Science reveals things immediately, unilaterally, and unconditionally. Thus when Laruelle refers to non-philosophy as a science of philosophy he means simply that it focuses on philosophy's radical or irreflective immanence, not its penchant for the transcendental.[55]

Science at its most generic is a model for non-philosophy. Like science, non-philosophy transcends examples. Science is a system of principles derived from experimentation and is never dependent on one set of examples. In non-philosophy, argument by example is displaced for a "scientific" reduction of the raw materials operative within a given text (or texts) of standard philosophy. Laruelle's move to resituate the philosophical project by casting it as an immanent science of Philosophical Decision enables a renewal of "realist" philosophy in the literal sense. Philosophy is seen "within the limits of reality and validity," writes Laruelle, "that henceforth science is alone able to define."[56] It is from this perspective—the perspective of a scientific "vision-in-One"—that philosophies are equalized. All philosophy is equally insufficient to capture and know the Real for the immanence that it is. Again, this immanent recasting of the philosophical field constitutes an *equality of thought* in a rigorously restricted sense. All philosophies are equal *only* inasmuch as they are equally insufficient to capture and decide the Real. But, as O'

Maoilearca notes, "philosophical views are not dismissed as failed representations. Rather, they and their 'limits' . . . are made Real, they are physicalized as parts of the Real."[57] O' Maoilearca's point is that the *positive contribution* of non-philosophy to philosophical discourse is to *materialize the limits of philosophy* and to show that these material limits are themselves Real and part of the Real. Non-philosophy thus possesses a strange theory of the Real beyond the axiom of the Real as closed to epistemic decisionism. The Real of non-philosophy is that of *philosophy's real limits*.

Another realism

There is a realist streak in non-philosophy, but of a kind scarcely recognizable within the frame of standard philosophical realism. The realism of non-philosophy is more like the realism of French painting of the mid-nineteenth century like that of Manet or Courbet. It was Manet, Courbet, and other painters of the Realist movement, whose gritty scenes of laborers, the poor, and sex workers exposed the limits of what passed for realist art by the standards of academic painting. The French Realists expanded the realist frame of art, and at the same time, exposed the limits imposed by a certain reification of the "beautiful" as the proper referent of "realist" painting. It was a critique of the standardization and ideological work done by that seemingly innocuous term "realism." Seen from the perspective of those thought to be unfit "subjects" of realist art, the French Realists elaborated a counter-discourse of the Real that demonstrated with startling (even scientific) clarity the material and cultural limits imposed on the Real by the standard philosophy of representationalist art, which at that time was ideologically intertwined with the classical aesthetics of beauty.

Likewise, the realism of standard philosophy decides what is real—atomic matter, will, power, class struggle, language, experience, among many others. Non-philosophy shows these "subjects" of realist philosophy to be products of philosophical decisions that materially enforce a closure of the Real. Thus, the realism of non-philosophy is not of a kind that would decide that realism is *the* sovereign perspective, but rather its realism is of a sort that demonstrates the *limits* of even those philosophies that appear most faithful to what is real. It shows then the work, the *philosophical* work, done by the term "philosophical realism," which renders its realism indistinguishable from the Real. The remainders and aporias of realism are thus the point of departure for a non-philosophical realism—a realism without philosophy—that makes Real and "physical" the limits enforced by "philosophical realism." And like the flatness of Manet's realism, the ontological flatness of the non-philosophical perspective yields a strange realism that is not that of resemblance and representationalism. Manet's realism was a realism true both to the conditions of material life *and* to the raw material facts of painting understood as the material application of paint to surface. His was a realism *of* painting. Likewise, the realism of non-philosophy realizes itself as a material practice of rendering real *the truth of the fiction* according to which standard representationalist philosophy is supposed to grasp and know the Real.

Having said all this, we must ask: What more is non-philosophy? What is it beyond its negation of standard philosophical decisionism? What can it produce? It is different, yes. But does it make a difference? How could we measure that difference and how might art speak in a parallel tongue to that difference? If non-philosophy is an art of writing—a *philo-fiction*—then what does this mean (if anything) for art's relation to philosophy? How to think or fictionalize the problematic of an *art of philosophy* rather than a standard philosophy of art? What is the "non" of non-philosophy and non-aesthetics? We will explore this in the next chapter.

2

"Non" is Not Negation

The "non" of non-philosophy has been its nemesis. Laruelle has frequently analogized the "non" of non-philosophy to the "non" of non-Euclidian geometry. As non-Euclidian geometry—a geometry of curved surfaces—does not *negate* the Euclidian geometry of flat surfaces, so non-philosophy is not a negation of standard philosophy. Non-philosophy, like non-Euclidian geometry, prescribes a different set of axioms. Standard philosophy axiomatically decides on the Real on the basis of its presupposed sufficiency to grasp and decide its nature. Non-philosophy, by contrast, axiomatically decides that it is not sufficient to grasp and decide the Real. The latter does not negate the former. Refusing the Principle of Sufficient Philosophy upon which standard philosophy justifies its practice of Philosophical Decision, non-philosophy begins with the principle of philosophical *insufficiency*, which brings a new focus and potency to other para-philosophical discourses and practices. We will explore some of these, including photography, art, and fiction. We will examine how the diverse practices of non-aesthetics draw on these "non-philosophical" or "para-philosophical" practices to orient its aims and hopes.

Foci

At its historical advent, photography was an art of stillness rather than temporal movement. Part of this had surely to do with the technological constraints at the time, which did not allow one to capture movement without blurring or entirely effacing the image. This technological constraint underwrote the construction of a standardized photographic aesthetics of focus in the form of sharply focused photographic images. The ideology of sharp focus led to the development of inventive compositing techniques (especially the use of multiple negatives) to produce and preserve the illusion of the sharply focused image and the aesthetic ideology that standardized it. Early photographers, such as Henry Peach Robinson, perfected darkroom techniques for compositing multiple negatives so as to produce, for example, group portraits set in seemingly uniform focus. This darkroom fiction helped to cement the emerging discourse of photography as a technologically enhanced form of visual empiricism. The "realism" of nineteenth-century photography was thus secured by an aesthetic frame that bound stillness to lifelikeness. But there were dissenters.

Julia Margaret Cameron (1815–79) was an English socialite. She came to photography late in life around the age of forty. But she took to photography quickly and in time established herself as a successful photographer by photographing the elite society of Victorian arts and letters such as Charles Darwin, Alfred Lord Tennyson, and others. But she also cultivated an impressive body of "art" photography that challenged the reigning conception of focus in the nineteenth century. To her many critics, Cameron's signature works appeared "blurry" or "unfocused." Many assumed that this was evidence of her lack of skill or training. But it wasn't. It was a conscious aesthetic choice. Cameron refused to use the props, rods and other supports that most photographers at the time used to keep their subjects still during the lengthy exposure time. She instead preferred to allow the trace of movement to appear in the final image. And she would intentionally adjust the focal field to accentuate the trace of movement. Her work presented a powerful aesthetic and theoretical counter-measure against the reigning convention of her day. Indeed, her work revealed the sharp focused aesthetic to be nothing more than a naturalized convention whose artifice ironically secured its claim to "realism."

Cameron came to see focus as a continuum rather than a binary. She saw photographic subjects as neither simply focused nor simply unfocused. Rather, Cameron aesthetically and theoretically resituated focus by pluralizing its potential and potency. She saw the problem of focus as the problem of *foci*. What she called her "first success" in this regard was a portrait of a young girl named Annie (Figure 4). The soft-focused image of the young girl speaks to the tenderness of Cameron's affection for her. But it also signifies the materiality of the medium of photography. Cameron's photograph (and many like it) show focus as a material registration of the working of the camera lens. It speaks to what is real in photography: the camera, photographer, and subject. And the streaks in the image speak to its chemical facticity. Cameron here as elsewhere allowed the wet plate to run slightly as the image solidified on its surface. What to many appeared as a blemish in the final image was for her the mark of a materialist aesthetic true to the materials at hand. Hers was a realism of the human body as a body of movement *and* a realism true

FIGURE 4 *Julia Margaret Cameron*, Annie, *1864*.
Source: Cameron, Julia Margaret (1815–79). Albumen silver print, 17.9 × 14.3 cm. Digital image courtesy of the Getty's Open Content Program.

to the material constraints and possibilities inherent in the medium of photography itself.

In 1864, Cameron published a short text, *Annals of My Glass House*, in which she charted her career and laid out reasons for her aesthetic choices. On the question of focus, she wrote, that "when focusing and coming to something that to my eye was very beautiful, I stopped instead of screwing on the lens to the more definite focus which all other photographers insist upon."[1] In private letters, Cameron was even more direct. She writes, "conventional Topographic Photography" can result only in "skeleton rendering of feature & form without that roundness & fullness of form and feature, that modeling of flesh and limb which the focus I use only can give."[2] Cameron identified the supreme artifice at the heart of the realist image of "conventional Topographic Photography": the living body is never still. Movement is life. That is why Barthes identified the stilled photographic image with death. "With the Photograph," writes Barthes, "we enter into *flat* Death."[3] The body in its corporeal "fullness" of "flesh and limb" is the axiomatic point of departure for Cameron's deployment of soft focus. Her photographic affirmation of the body of movement and the materiality of photography represents an entirely different conception of photographic realism than that conventionalized by the stilled body manufactured by nineteenth-century studio constraints such as neck braces and back-straightening rods or through darkroom manipulation. Cameron's soft-focused work *brings into focus* the artifice of the still and sharply focused image of standard nineteenth-century photography.[4]

Cameron's soft-focus work is an "art of negation," to borrow a poignant phrase from Andrew Hass's study of Hegel, for it negates the standard practice of focus in nineteenth-century photography.[5] But it is an *art* of negation and not a simple opposition. Cameron's concept of focus displaces the binary logic of nineteenth-century focus. Her art of negation founds a new axiomatic. The body in motion and the materiality of photography constitute an entirely new order of photographic aesthetics. Cameron's photographic art of negation has a parallel structure to the logic of non-aesthetics. It is not that Cameron is a case study in Laruellean non-aesthetics. Rather, her work and his parallel one another inasmuch as each works with the "raw material" of their media to challenge the standard aesthetic conventions that regulate practice within each. I acknowledge that I am here freely cloning some raw material from Hass's study of Hegel because his concept of the "art of negation" postulates dialectics as a doing. Hass notes that the intelligibility of the concept of "negation" since Hegel has suffered at the hands of its seeming synonym—the "negative." A negative, like a negative balance in a bank account, is chiefly linked to absence. But negation is not an absence but an act. Hass writes:

> The suffix "-ion" denotes a verbal action made into a noun or made, we might say, objective, perhaps even concrete. The act of negating, then, finds its object or concretion in negation, yet not in any static way, but in a manner by which the action continues even in its nominalization. Negation then becomes the actual or actualized activity. . . . Negation actualizes by doing. Negation *does*.[6]

Cameron's work is at once an act and an art for it did not simply negate the nineteenth-century photographic dialectic of "in focus" or "out of focus." It transformed the dialectical field of focus itself. She came to see that the aesthetic question of focus was also a question of power. It was not a matter of aesthetics pure and simple, for nothing that is culturally naturalized is ever categorically simple and pure but by its nature involves a whole set of complex "extrinsic" factors. Cameron was keenly aware of the "amphibology" of aesthetics. Behind the façade of the nineteenth-century aesthetic ideal of "art for art's sake" lay a disavowed knowledge/power structure reinforced by the naturalization of institutional practices within the academy and the art world. As Cameron noted in a revealing letter: "What is focus and who has the right to say what is the legitimate focus?"[7] Cameron identified the twinned problem of "legitimate focus" and "who has the right to say what is the legitimate focus" as both an aesthetic question and matter of cultural and institutional legitimation.

The institutionalization of sharp focus was carried out through a patriarchal photographic establishment that greeted Cameron's challenge as a form of aesthetic and socio-political-sexual subversion of their institutional legitimacy. As Lindsay Smith has powerfully demonstrated, the phallogocentric authority invested in sharp focus followed a pattern of thought whose lineage can be traced to the advent of philosophical modernity epitomized by Descartes's insistence on "clear and distinct ideas" and Spinoza's "geometral" model of philosophical argumentation. The modern convention of philosophical argument by clear axioms and sharply derived proofs underwrote a sexual bias for the language of clarity and sharp focus as the sole legitimate language of modern "philosophical man." What Deleuze might call the modern "image of thought" was that of a man mentally picturing the world through a geometral and perspectival grid. This grid functioned as a mirror of the patriarchal desire to see the world "philosophically" and to be seen by the world, as a man with the power to see in this way. The geometral model of philosophical reflection was reproduced in transposed aesthetic form in early photography. "From the beginning," writes Lindsay Smith, "the photographic definition of focus was made to serve existing systems of visual representation, and in particular to conspire with the dominance of geometral perspective" typical of authoritative philosophy of the day.[8] Cameron's art of negation thus provided an alternative visual and epistemic point of departure.

Cameron's challenge was a "non-philosophical" challenge to the reigning ideology of nineteenth-century aesthetics. Her art of negation, as I use the term here, is a dual action: it cancels and transforms what it opposes. Cameron's art of negation reconfigured the whole of photography through the medium of focus. Photography (not merely focus) is transformed: a new axiomatic is posited. It is by virtue of this art of negation that Cameron found a new freedom outside the philo-geometral structures and strictures of patriarchal visuality. Cloning some additional material from Hass, we can ask: "Where does one get the freedom to invent freedom?"[9] Answer: "Only from a negation that first negates the constituting freedom in order to allow the constructed freedom to arise."[10] Cameron's reconstruction of photographic practice is a "constructed freedom" founded on the creative negation (if not creative destruction) of the "constituting freedom" constituted by the patriarchal foundation and normalization of sharp focus. The early photographic establishment could not "see" Cameron's photography *as photography*. It was in this sense what Laruelle might call an instance of "non-photography" or "non-standard photography."

The aesthetics of aesthetics

Cameron's art of negation provides a fitting entry point into our discussion of the focus of non-aesthetics. Laruelle's axiom that standard philosophy of art obscures the philosophy immanent to art itself is most forcefully elaborated in his texts on photography. In *The Concept of Non-Photography* and *Photo-Fiction*, Laruelle seeks a creative negation of the standard subordination of art to philosophy. He takes art as a model for thought and not as its subject. But this gesture is more than a mere inversion. To take art as model, and not as subject, is to practice a form of writing that aims to be creative *and* critical. What is at once creative and critical about non-aesthetics is also true of Laruelle's other non-philosophical practices. Each in its own way parallels what it theorizes and theorizes that very parallelism. In other words, the subjects of non-philosophy are ultimately self-referential. It is like a closed circuit. Non-philosophy as a strategy and style of writing circuits through its subjects only to return to itself. What is to be determined or decided in non-philosophical prose is the style and strategy of resistance to Philosophical Decision.

There is an irony at the heart of Laruelle's project of non-philosophy. Non-philosophy's principal concern is a deeply philosophical concern. Indeed, Laruelle's critics will charge that non-philosophy is still philosophy. Anthony Paul Smith discusses this criticism in light of Laruelle's work on politics. It is worth quoting at length.

> Laruelle's critics take the ease with which "non" comes to the tips of Laruelle's fingers as he writes to be a sign that non-philosophy does not have anything to add to philosophical discourse. I am not interested here in arguing for Laruelle's place in the parliament of philosophy, where he can join with this or that party in the interminable debates of parliamentary philosophy. For, to stick with this metaphor of a parliament, such debates are always framed by rules taken to externally structure those parties. If one wants to be an *authentic* politician, then one follows these rules, one allows them to structure the debates, and, except in very rare cases of revolution, the structure of those debates is never up for debate. The logic of the "non" includes a refusal of the frame as

frame, instead treating that frame as entirely part of the material and actors that the frame claims to condition.[11]

Smith astutely evades the trap of defending Laruelle's philosophical significance in the "parliament of philosophy" for the very good reason that Laruelle's work precisely contests the normalization of the "rules" that "structure" standard philosophical discourse. And if it is only in "rare cases of revolution" that the structure of the debate becomes a matter of debate, then non-philosophy may be precisely a revolutionary instance in which the "frame" of philosophy is reframed and its material and discursive effects are questioned, challenged, and debated. Yet this would not be quite accurate, for non-philosophy does not propose bringing that debate to the floor of the "parliament of philosophy" to extend Smith's metaphor. It proposes exiting the parliament for what Adorno might call a "creative praxis" of philosophy.

Non-aesthetics is not a thinking "on" art; it is *an art of thinking* modeled on the immanent thought *in* art. Laruelle's creative practice indexes what I identify as the *twofold problem of the aesthetics of aesthetics.* Every writer who writes about art faces this twofold problem: What philosophical or historical frames of reference ought to frame the discussion and *what form of writing should be used?* The writer on aesthetics (like any writer) consciously or not adopts an aesthetics of writing. This twofold problem of the aesthetics of aesthetics is central to Laruelle's work. His "philo-fictions" of art self-consciously work in this twofold way. They are at once fictions of art and an art of fiction. First-time readers of Laruelle's work on art may well find this twofold aesthetics of aesthetics confusing. But it is not without precedent. It is important to historically contextualize Laruelle's work in this regard for it tempers the apparent strangeness of his work but it also serves to highlight what is unique in Laruelle's approach to this twofold problem. I want to then place Laruelle in a constellation of inventive writers on art: Theodor Adorno, Walter Benjamin, and Jacques Derrida. I have chosen these writers because they exhibit important tendencies and tensions present in Laruelle's work. I have grouped these tendencies and tensions under three headings: "abstract," "experimental," and "autonomous."

Abstract (Adorno)

Adorno was the chief aesthetician of the first generation of the Frankfurt School. He was professionally trained in philosophy and music. His musical tutor was Anton Webern who himself had trained under Arnold Schoenberg. The latter revolutionized music by rendering dissonance and atonality systematic by the "twelve-tone technique" (a technique by which all twelve tones of the Western scale are sounded once before any is sounded twice). Adorno's training in modernist musical composition was decisive for the development of his style of philosophical composition. His mature work represents a kind of "atonal philosophy" in the words of Martin Jay.[12] Likewise, Adorno's "negative dialectics" prizes irresolution over and against Hegelian harmonies.

In *Aesthetic Theory*, Adorno frames modernist art in prose that is as rigorously abstract and non-representational as modernist art itself. The hermeticism of modernist art is read by Adorno as the sign of art's disconnection from the commodified life-world of administered domination. Modernist art is "autonomous" for it is composed solely of its own immanent materiality as is especially evident in paintings about paint and surface, music about sound and silence, and literature about signs. Autonomous art is a sign of freedom that negatively indexes all that is not free under capital. "For absolute freedom in art," writes Adorno, "comes into contradiction with the unfreedom of the whole."[13] "The *meaning* of the artwork's autonomy," writes Geoff Boucher in his study of Adorno, "is that it self-legislates; that is, that it absorbs social and natural raw materials into its substance and converts them into artistic content under the law of form."[14] The autonomous work of art for Adorno contains a kernel of utopian hope. It signals the possibility of freedom under conditions of unfreedom. "In an almost totally reified society," writes Boucher, "autonomous art has become the last refuge of that creative practice which points beyond alienated labor."[15]

Aesthetic Theory is an aesthetic work on aesthetics. It confronts headlong the twofold problem. The paratactic tenor of Adorno's style of writing exemplifies a non-representationalist philosophy and a non-representationalist aesthetic that prizes the partial and discontinuous over and against representationalist totalities. One can literally see this on every page of the book. As Robert Hullot-Kentor observes:

> Opening to any page, without bothering to read a word, one sees that the book is visibly antagonistic. No one from the land of edutainment would compose these starkly unbeckoning sheer sides of type, uninterrupted by chapter titles or typographic markers, that have severed and jettisoned every approach and patched over most every apparent handhold.[16]

The forebodingly abstract nature of *Aesthetic Theory* owes its form to "autonomous art." The "visibly antagonistic" character of the text parallels non-representationalist art's antagonistic struggle against capital's imperative of easy consumption. Hullot-Kentor continues:

> The book's stylistic peculiarities derive from what makes *Aesthetic Theory* inimical to an American context; that it is oriented not to its readers but to the thing-in-itself. This is not, as will be immediately suspected, motivated by indifference to its readers. On the contrary, the book makes itself remote from its consumption out of interest in, and by its power of, self-immersion.[17]

Aesthetic Theory and the modernist art it frames are both inwardly focused on their immanent materiality. *Aesthetic Theory* accompanies or parallels as much as it comments on modernist art.

The abstraction of Adorno's aesthetics is echoed in much of Laruelle's work. In *The Concept of Non-Photography*, Laruelle articulates an abstract or "non-figurative" theory of photography derived from the immanent abstraction of photography itself. Jettisoning the nineteenth-century ideology of photography as a mirror reflection of the visible world, Laruelle seizes on the materiality of the *photo as photo* in its naked abstraction. The materiality of photography can only be accessed, Laruelle suggests, by an approach that resists the representationalist metaphysics of reflection. Laruelle writes:

> The task of a rigorous thought is . . . to found—at least in principle—an abstract theory of photography—but radically abstract, absolutely non-worldly and non-perceptual. Traditional, that is

to say merely philosophical, interpretations of photography are made on the basis of . . . the eye, the camera and its techniques, the object and the theme, the choice of object, of the scene, of the event. That is, they are made on the basis of semiology or phenomenology, doctrines that start out by ceding too much to the World . . . by interpreting it too quickly in relation to the transcendence of the World. . . . They found themselves on the faith in perception supposedly at the basis of the photographic act. But perhaps, fundamental to the latter, there is more than a faith, there is a veritable spontaneous photographic knowledge that must be described.[18]

A "rigorous" theory of photography (and we might add art) must, for Laruelle, resist the fall into the World as imaged in philosophical reflection. A theory of photography misses the "spontaneous photographic knowledge" contained in photography itself if it is bound up with concerns for the camera, the object, techniques, and visual perception. The immanent knowledge within photography given in the *photo as photo* (and not as double of the World) materially distances itself from the World as imaged in standard representationalist philosophies of photography. Like Adorno before him, Laruelle sees the abstract nature of his object as an immanent sign of freedom from the World ordered and dominated by dominant philosophies from economics to epistemology. Laruelle and Adorno's texts exhibit a non-representationalist aesthetic of writing on aesthetics modeled on the emancipatory aesthetics of autonomous art.

Experimental (Benjamin)

Benjamin circulated on the periphery of the Frankfurt School. He was undoubtedly its most experimental writer. Fusing philosophy with art, literature, politics, and religion, Benjamin's mature style of writing was modeled on surrealism. Juxtaposition, montage, readymades, photographs, fragments: Benjamin marshaled these objects and techniques into a surrealist-inspired mode of theoretical writing he called "dialectical images." His studies of art, literature, and photography immanently informed the imagistic character of his writing. History ceased to be a domain of finished finalities. It was for him a deposit of raw materials with which to image dialectical contrasts capable of illuminating the present. The "true image of the past," can only be grasped, Benjamin notes, as an "image that flashes-up in the moment of its recognizability."[19] Reading the dialectic of past and present as a dialectic of images, Benjamin strikes surrealist sparks: "The past carries a secret index by which it is referred to redemption. Doesn't a breath of the air that invaded earlier days caress us as well?"[20] Benjamin's stilled images juxtapose breath, touch, and time, finding a secret index of a past that is waiting to be reborn in the present. There is "a secret agreement," writes Benjamin, "between past generations and the present one."[21] And if this is so, then, for Benjamin, it must mean that "our coming was expected on earth."[22] The past waits for the coming of a "weak messianic" present to redeem its suffering.

In the images that flash up in Benjamin's creative prose, we recognize the present from Benjamin's "weak messianic" perspective. This messianic vision is made in and through the image. Benjamin's images hit the mind's eye with the speed of film. Benjamin's prose compresses and condenses standard philosophies of time and events into quasi-filmic space and time. He finds in the aesthetics of surrealism non-standard philosophical resources to think within and beyond the realm of art. Benjamin's "desire to render philosophy surrealistic," writes Richard Wolin, was an effort to "reduce the discrepancy between philosophical thought and everyday life."[23] Wolin is right to an extent. But for the surrealists "everyday life" was stranger than we know. The strangeness of everyday life according to the surrealists lies behind the facade of administered normality and ideological certainties. The surrealists sought to awaken their audiences to the strangeness of everyday life. They sought to rid thought of the complacency of common sense. Surrealism challenged the pragmatic intuitionism of habituated thought that thinks itself sufficient to grasp the reality of the everyday. This is why Marxism and surrealism, for Benjamin, are intellectual cousins. Both are committed to piercing the veil of naturalized conditions to reveal the strange mechanisms that operate behind our backs. Shock was the method. Benjamin's writing operationalizes a methodological aesthetics of shock to "divest" the world of its "familiarity and thereby stir the reader from a state of passivity into an active and critical posture."[24] Benjamin's style of philosophical aesthetics clones the aesthetics of surrealism in order to produce less a theory of surrealism than a surrealistic philosophy to awaken his readers from the slumbers induced by standard philosophy.

Benjamin's surrealist philosophy of juxtaposition bears comparison with Laruelle's non-philosophy of superposition. The dialectical image contrasts of Benjamin's writings and the quantic collisions of Laruelle's "generic science" are efforts to open philosophy to a new vision radically different than that which is reflected in philosophy's narcissistic mirror. The imagistic aesthetic of Benjamin's writing indexes what *does not appear* in the representationalist frame of thinking. His dialectical images awaken us to what we do not see. The "real" world obscures the Real we do not see and know. Laruelle uses imagery in a similar fashion. His images are drawn from the world of quantum physics, art, and philosophy. But these images produce a non-representationalist theory on the order of a kind of abstract-surrealism of science. Consider these lines by Laruelle from *Photo-Fiction*:

> Non-standard aesthetics is not founded upon the substitution of the Principle of Sufficient Philosophy with the Principle of Sufficient Mathematics (we hardly gain anything by that sleight of hand), but upon its substitution with a mathematics that is itself decontextualized or reduced to several algebraic equations. When compared to this matrix, standard aesthetics itself appears retroactively restrained and founded upon the ultimate philosophical inclination [i.e., Philosophical Decision], the double intervention of transcendence or the context of the Principle of Sufficient Philosophy, a first time as interpreting in a dominant manner its technological core of art, a second time as an index tilting this set toward its philosophical destination or confirming it or re-affirming it.[25]

The mathematics of non-aesthetics is surrealistic, which Laruelle places under the sign of the "Principle of Sufficient Mathematics." Non-standard mathematics is radically "decontextualized." Its aim is to retroactively discover how the object of standard aesthetics is *derived* as if it were a mathematical result. Non-aesthetics sees standard aesthetics as enclosing the whole of art into a quasi-mathematical "set" determined by standard axioms of beauty, aesthetic pleasure, the history of styles and techniques. The set-theory of standard aesthetics auto-confirms a preset equation. Art equals art where "art" is defined as the set of all things determined to be art by Philosophical Decision.

The aesthetics of aesthetics as practiced by Adorno, Benjamin, and Laruelle with its paratactic condensations and surrealistic flashes is radically abstract. Even its imagistic dimension is non-representationalist in the last instance. Their work is modeled on the negative and revolutionary condition of avant-garde art. "Reading a piece by Adorno or Benjamin," notes Jay, "brings to mind a comment the filmmaker Jean-Luc Goddard is once said to have made when asked if his films had a beginning, a middle, and an end. 'Yes,' he replied, 'but not necessarily in that order.'"[26] Jay astutely underscores the aesthetic significance of Benjamin and Adorno's writing on aesthetics. And this is no less true of Laruelle's work. (As we noted, Laruelle himself attributes his entrance into philosophy as in part a response to a film by Antonioni.)

Autonomy (Derrida)

The dialectical correlate to "autonomous art" is "autonomous theory." The effort to aestheticize philosophy secures a parallel autonomy for the critical act. "The reciprocal autonomy of art and theory," writes Laruelle, "signifies that we [theorists] have a claim to 'creation.'"[27] The non-standard art theorist recognizes the freedom in art without subjugating that freedom by turning it into a subject of philosophical reflection. Let us explore the concept of *autonomous theory* through a comparative study of Derrida and Laruelle.

In a collection of essays, *The Truth in Painting*, Derrida reframes the standard relation between art and criticism. The last essay of the collection, "Cartouches," was written as the catalog essay for an exhibition of sixty-one drawings of a small coffin-like object by the artist Gérard Titus-Carmel at the Museum of Modern Art at the Centre Pompidou in April 1978.

Derrida's essay parallels drawing in general. It does not seek to reproduce or reflect Carmel-Titus's drawings specifically. Derrida works around the edges of the artist's drawings like a frame. The essay thus calls attention to its own status as a framing device by breaking the frame and exploiting the gap between frame and work. The title of the essay is telling. A "cartouche" is an ancient Egyptian hieroglyph identifiable by its unique form: a horizontal oval flanked on one side by a solid line. The hieroglyphic form fascinates Derrida as it offers endless room to play on the dehiscence between the graphic and vocal aspects of the sign as well as providing a historical inroad to deconstruct the boundary between visuality and textuality. Moreover, the ancient Egyptian hieroglyph's embeddedness in the collective mythos of the pharaonic culture of death, funerary rites, and the afterlife intersect with Derrida's insistence on the link between writing, tracing, and archiving as part and parcel of the work of dying, death, mourning, and haunting.

"Cartouches" functions as a para-text to Titus-Carmel's work. It is not only that Derrida's essay stylistically and substantially deconstructs the boundary between creation and critique; what is equally significant is the way in which the text catalyzes a meta-critique of the domination of art by philosophy, theory, and criticism. Derrida sought a measure of critical distance not only from the art of Titus-Carmel but importantly also from the standard temptation to judge art. His essay on Titus-Carmel does not "quote," "paraphrase," or "frame" the work of the artist. Rather, he models his essay on the principles of *line-work* by drawing it into the syntax of his prose. Drawing (as represented in the work of Titus-Carmel) is taken as the model (*not the object*) of Derrida's critical act. Derrida's text creates a para-text to drawing in general or in a generic sense. The *line* of Derrida's text—its fits, starts, sketchiness—clones the thought processes immanently inscribed within the art of drawing. His meta-drawing, *a drawing of the line of criticism through drawing*, metaphorically parallels the "coffins" of Titus-Carmel inasmuch as they project a work of internment, marking, like a grave, the authority of philosophy over the meaning and significance of art. Derrida writes:

If I am writing for the dumbstruck "spectators" whom this concerns . . . I must not free them from fascination by my discourse. For I mean that discourse not to meddle with anything (the thing you're looking at is not my business or that of my discourse which it can very well do without), I mean it not to touch anything. It concerns you . . . leave it alone with you, remain silent when all is said and done . . . pass to one side of it in silence, like another theory, another series, say nothing of what it represents for me, nor even for him. And at the same stroke . . . leave it, the thing to the nameless crypt of its mutism.[28]

A theory opens here that envisions criticism as a para-discourse: *critique as parallelism*. It is "another theory" and an act of criticism, which parallels the "thing you're looking at," but as for the work itself, Derrida notes, this "is not my business." Derrida's discourse leaves the art "alone" via a parallel movement of passing "to one side of it." In this passing to one side, Derrida passes over without eclipsing the silence—the "mutism"—of Titus's Carmel's deathly silent works. The title of Derrida's parallel interventions (for there is not one intervention at issue)—"Cartouches"—is properly pluralized for it parallels a "set" of "drawings" that insistently pressure the singular frame inscribed in the term "set," and the singularly specific term "drawings." Derrida continues, Titus-Carmel "says 'drawings,' a 'large number of drawings,' but they are not solely drawings; there are watercolors, gouaches, engravings, and the set, including *the princeps, the coffin itself*, what is it a set of? What does set mean here?"[29] What is the princeps of these "drawings" (if that is the word)? What is the first of the order? Is there an order? Titus-Carmel's "drawings" are apparently based on a small, miniature, coffin-like object reproduced in photographic form in the text. This coffin-like thing has many elements or articles that do not correspond to commonsense notions of "coffin" such as the loop of string that sits where a body should and which also spills out of a number of holes around its edges. These are more than mere details. They breach the borders of the term "coffin" and lead us "dumbstruck spectators" to question what we are looking at versus what we read in the title of the exhibition. Between words and things falls the shadow.

Derrida's text parallels the iterative and processual nature of drawing *and* writing. Each of Titus-Carmel's "drawings" is signed with a month and a year. Derrida parallels this in his text with a series of dated entries that mark a thought that evolves over time. Each "time" he writes, Derrida clones the temporal continuities and discontinuities that mark the making of a set or a body of work. The disjunctive distances and abrupt changes in direction that course through his temporal itinerary of writings pressure the stable frame of the "essay" as a singular and discrete form. The daily entries inscribe a metanarrative of the continuance of life (if not thought). This iterative process of living disjunctively parallels the thematic of death inscribed in the coffin-like drawings. Every day could be the last for the writer (or the artist). Derrida's entry for December 4, 1977 reads in part:

> What can one desire of a coffin if not to have it for one's own, to steal it, to put oneself inside it and see oneself in it, lie or give birth in it . . . preferably with the other, this being another way of neutralizing it, of calming one's own terror, of dealing with alterity, of wearing down alterity. . . . But what can one desire of a coffin except that it remain where it is, at a distance, to one side . . . that it remain the other's?[30]

To put death to one side, to keep it close as one keeps close one's enemy, refigures the problematic of parallelism and critique through the last figure of life—death. Each day marks a moment where death can be put to one side—forgotten momentarily—only to resurface anxiously like an unquiet grave. How to put to death the anxiety of death? Titus-Carmel's coffin-like figures frame death through an art of imprecision and approximation. Who knows what death really looks like? Who really knows how to represent or mark it? How can death be marked or turned into a mark of art?

The lines of Derrida's "Cartouches" are drawn through the schism of sign and picture, criticism and art, within and without, life and death. But it is also a drawing of the line through the figure of the "cartouche"—the hieroglyph that is at once sign and picture—image and text. It is not simply that the textual/visual opposition is deconstructed. It is redrawn and resignified iteratively through a line that is not merely "drawn" but by "drawings." Each dated "cartouche" or "drawing" archives a processual movement disjunctively adjoined to the next iteration of line segment or instance of drawing. Drawing here comes to mean indefinite duration and not a discretely ordered and bordered pictorial form or formulation. In the composite of Titus-

Carmel/Derrida, lines are timelines marking disjunctive topoi and temporalities.

The iterative temporality of Derrida's "Cartouches," and Titus-Carmel's "drawings," opens at once within an aesthetic and ethical horizon. For each new time, and the disjunctions it brings about, renews the alterity of the work of writing and drawing in one stroke. Each look at the model, the subject, the theme in either case (Derrida or Titus-Carmel) opens a new frame and reconstitutes the strangeness of the "subject" in a mode of enunciation that repeats differentially across the sequence or set. The relation between Derrida's work and that of Titus-Carmel's cannot be adequately framed by stable narrative relations between art and critique. Something else emerges in the interstices of times and the lines that mark them. The relation between the two is set by the rhythms of iteration as a mode of marking and address. "Derrida has consistently drawn on the logic of iterability," writes David Wills, "to address, always from a different perspective and in a different format, the structural and conceptual aporias that that logic gives rise to."[31]

The aporias of the text/image problematic that surface iteratively within the couplet Derrida/Titus-Carmel meta-critically signifies the aporetic nature of the frame. It is the persistence, and the persistently unresolved, tension between sign and mark inscribed and encrypted within the Derrida/Titus-Carmel structure that marks the making of the work as a work of alterity and liberates both work and word from a dominant telos. Iteration bridges the aesthetical and ethical dimensions. The repetition, always with a difference in each case, restores and reconstitutes the defamiliarizing function of Derrida's aesthetics of aesthetics. The frame (contra Kant) is central despite its peripheral location. For the frame organizes the recognizability of art as art. Like Derrida, Laruelle's non-aesthetics operationalizes a meta-critical thinking of the *frame as frame* as at once an aesthetic and philosophical problematic.

The work of Adorno, Benjamin, and Derrida provide important historical parallels for Laruelle's inventive work. But, as I've suggested, we can also see these figures as "conceptual personae" that operate within Laruelle's corpus. The abstract (Adorno), experimental (Benjamin), and autonomous (Derrida) aspects of Laruelle's work function like a matrix of tendencies and tensions that organize his non-representationalist theory of aesthetics through an aesthetic fictionalizing of standard philosophical art criticism. Reading Laruelle in his own terms as "fiction" enables us to see his work as paralleling, in theory, the utopian aspiration of truly autonomous art.

Conversionary surfaces

We can further examine the immanence of aesthetics—the aesthetics of aesthetics—through the adjacent concept of "surface." Adorno, Benjamin, Derrida, and Laruelle seize upon the twofold problem of the aesthetics of aesthetics. Aesthetics for them never stands outside a certain *aesthetic relation to the very question of aesthetics itself*. Their work offers an immanent theory of aesthetics as a condition that is always already prior to any thought on aesthetics. The media of marks—sign or picture, volumetric object, or volume of text, or what Laruelle calls a "theoretical installation"—iteratively restages the problematic of aesthetics as an immanent condition prior to its designation as an attribute or problem of art. The practice of aesthetics for these writers is a problem of drawing lines and framing writing's aesthetic relation to aesthetic reflection. Their writing presents aesthetics as an irreducible and immanent surface of philosophical aesthetics.

Philosophical Decision in the arena of art relies on its constitutive blindness to the immanence of aesthetics. Let me clarify this point with a clear example from the archives of American Abstract Expressionism of the mid-twentieth century. It's not the art I want to focus on here but its critical reception. At the very moment that painters such as Jackson Pollock, Mark Rothko, and Barnett Newman were redefining the landscape of abstract art in America, their most vocal champion, Clement Greenberg, was transforming art criticism. He argued in reviews and essays that Abstract Expressionism had realized the material "essence" of painting as nothing more or less than paint and surface.[32] He prized the aesthetic of "flatness" in modernist painting above all for it appeared to confirm the material reality of the painted surface *as surface* and not illusory space. Greenberg's dictum that *surface is surface and paint is paint* secured a seemingly self-evident materialist basis for aesthetics. But, as

Jacques Rancière argues in "Painting in the Text," Greenberg's *materialist surface* is a *conceptual surface* whose conceptuality is organized by a certain historical "regime" that regulated the relation between seeing and saying.

Rancière draws out the normative and selective framing of "medium," "materiality," and "surface" in the articulation of Greenbergian modernist aesthetics. "A medium is not a 'proper' means or material," writes Rancière, it "is a surface of conversion: a surface of equivalence between the different arts' ways of making; a conceptual space of articulation between these ways of making and forms of visibility and intelligibility determining the way in which they can be viewed and conceived."[33] Greenberg's "surface" is a "surface of conversion" for it converts the materiality and medium-specificity of painting into "flatness," "paint," and "essence."

Rancière uncovers the *aesthetic frame* that structures the appearance of Greenberg's materialist and formalist criticism. This aesthetic or meta-aesthetic layer lies in the precise distribution of the relations between the discursive and the visible which Greenbergian modernism draws into an equivalence: on one side "medium," "paint," "surface," and "flatness," is rendered equivalent to "material" and "essence" on the other. The *conceptual surface* on which this equivalence is inscribed is non-representationalist and set in place by a rigorous geometry of reduction: it is the critico-aesthetic double of the style of art that Greenberg championed. "The surface claimed as the specific medium of pure painting," continues Rancière, "is in fact a different medium. It is the theatre of a de-figuration/denomination."[34] "Materiality," "medium," "flatness," "essence" do not comprise a bedrock for a materialist aesthetics of painting. These are merely the raw materials that organize the Greenbergian aesthetic "surface of conversion." Rancière's reading intersects with what we have already identified as the "aesthetics of aesthetics." This problematic is self-consciously underscored in Laruelle's theory "fictions."

Laruelle's "fictions" are not without precedent as we saw with Baudrillard. And indeed, the experimental impulse marks the work of modernist and postmodernist writers on the arts from Benjamin to Derrida. But this impulse is far more visible in postmodern critical theory. Gregory Ulmer was among the first to take notice of this stylistic shift. In his landmark essay, "The Object of Post-Criticism," Ulmer sees the experimental styles of postmodern theory as the critical clone of the avant-gardist aesthetics of modernist art. Ulmer writes:

> What is at stake in the controversy surrounding contemporary critical writing is easier to understand when placed in the context of modernism and postmodernism in the arts. The issue is "representation"—specifically the representation of the object of study in a critical text. Criticism is now being transformed in the same way that literature and the arts were transformed by the avant-garde movements in the early decades of . . . [the twentieth century]. The break with "mimesis," with the values and assumptions of "realism," which revolutionized the modernist arts, is now underway (belatedly) in criticism.[35]

Ulmer's point concerning the belated influence of avant-gardist aesthetics on critical writing should not be passed over quickly. It is not only important that criticism underwent an avant-gardist turn; it is also of equal importance that this turn was *belated*. Modernist criticism of the Greenbergian school appears from Ulmer's "post-critical" vantage to be less the high-water mark of modernism than a hinge point on the boundary of the *postmodern practice of criticism*. The aesthetics of modernist art soon enough breached the citadel of criticism at once revealing and transforming the aesthetic dimension of aesthetic theory that had been there all along. Laruelle's experimental work is surely part of the history of this belated migration of avant-gardist aesthetics from modernist art to postmodern criticism. In Laruelle's work, this migration takes the form of the procedure of cloning the aesthetics of art into an aesthetics of theory in that shadows, mimes, and revoices the materiality of philosophy in an aesthetic register voided of the decisionist dynamic of standard aesthetics.

Cloning

Laruelle's art-fictions are composed of clones—concepts taken from standard philosophy—but voided of their bearing on the "nature" of art. These cloned fictions clone the resistance to the Real embodied in the concept of literary fiction itself. This is why it is hard to "use"

Laruelle's fictive clones to *do* art theory in the standard sense. Cloning is a creative activity like artmaking itself. It makes concepts into characters or conceptual personae that "speak" in a non-decisionist voice. Thus, readers of non-philosophy will spot many words in Laruelle's work that look exactly like philosophical concepts they have encountered elsewhere. But these concepts are clones that are immanently (and self-referentially) determined by the style and syntax of non-philosophy. This can be frustrating because we are used to reading philosophy in the standard way by identifying concepts and then seeing how they work with respect to the Real. But Laruelle's clones don't work in that way. Indeed, they do not seem to relate to anything but non-philosophy. I myself first found this quite annoying. Everything seems to return to the term "non-philosophy." But this relentlessly self-referential character of Laruelle's writing is itself a stylistic clone of the Real. This requires some unpacking.

Recall that Laruelle works from the perspective of "vision-in-One"—a view that posits the Real as One and foreclosed to philosophical grasp. The Real as One exceeds philosophical grasp since philosophy cannot conceptualize the univocity of the Real without splitting it into what is philosophically intelligible and not. But the One is not two. Just as everything is immanent to the Real, so too are the clones of non-philosophy immanent to it. To be sure, thought too is immanent to the Real, but for Laruelle thought can neither know nor determine the Real. Rather, the Real is determinant of all thought (philosophical and non-philosophical). Thought does not relate to the Real, for the Real does not relate to anything for it is precisely the all that is. Thus, the Real only has a *relation of non-relation* to thought. The clone, then, is an approximate form—a fiction—that models the non-relationality of thought to the Real by its relentlessly self-referential determination by non-philosophy. Put more simply: non-philosophy determines the immanent and self-referential character of its clones in a way that parallels (or itself clones) the Real's immanent determination on all thought. In *Principles of Non-Philosophy*, Laruelle writes:

> The theory of cloning is . . . fundamental within a thought which is nonetheless not one of identity in the philosophical and intentional sense, but a thought *by* and *according to* identity. More exactly, a thinking *in-identity*. Indeed, the formula "in-One" which we use

[and] . . . finds itself within the expression "in-the-last-instance" . . . does not designate an effective inherence in the Real and still less a process within the Real. . . . "In-One" identically means the transcendental clone as received by way of the One but not constitutive of it.[36]

The prose is tortured in part because Laruelle's syntax aims at describing the clone and the cloning procedure without reifying it into a standard philosophical concept. The "transcendental" dimension of the clone does not designate some conceptual heaven removed from the embeddedness of immanence. Rather the term "transcendental" is a structural marker that designates the clone as that which transcends the profile of standard philosophical conceptualization. The clone is not a concept. It has neither the conceptual solidity of a concept nor the semantic clarity of a word. It transcends the bounds of the word and the concept, and is thus, in this sense, "transcendental" or, as Derrida would say, "quasi-transcendental."

Cloning is a way of thinking the radically singular quality of the Real as determinant in the last instance. The Real is all that is and is, therefore, something that strangely we have no relation to. This surely sounds odd. But for there to be a relation there has to be a distance. There has to be something *to* which one relates. But there is nothing to relate *to* in the case of the Real. The Real is all that is and is therefore immanent to all relations. The only relation to the Real is that of *non-relation*. Smith explains that the significance of the sign "clone" for Laruelle is that it is distinct from the conceptual and metaphysical trappings of reflection. The "clone is not a mere copy of an original," Smith writes, nor "is it a reflection upon something other than it. The clone retains its own identity . . . but carries the same genetic structure as the material it is cloned from."[37] The clone signifies the "unilateral" causality of the Real as One without positing a form of reflective conceptualization that would presuppose a relation of philosophy to the Real. Non-philosophical thought in this restricted sense has no relation to the Real just as a clone is a parallel or double of its progenitor and thereby retains its own immanent *identity as a clone* (and not a mere copy).

John O' Maoilearca explains cloning by way of another closely related analogy: miming and charades. "Perhaps a more suitable analogue for . . . cloning," writes O' Maoilearca, "comes in an alternative to the 'philosophical game of positions': the non-philosophical game of charades."[38] Where philosophy takes a position via a decision on the Real, non-philosophy transacts a charade of postures that mime philosophy but strips it of its decisional authoritarianism. Non-philosophy is a shadow of standard philosophy or even a shadow-play, but its critical edge is preserved by clarifying the structural profile of standard philosophy. "Such a charade," O' Maoilearca concludes, is "a mime that engages the whole of philosophy while at the same time (re)viewing it in a new light: . . . Nothing is destroyed, deconstructed, or negated. Everything is reviewed, mimed, or 'postured.'"[39]

Non-philosophy is not a negation of standard philosophy any more than a clone is a negation of that which it is cloned from. Non-philosophy is a figure that *parallels* philosophy like a shadow, but which has its own immanent identity. Photography (as noted earlier) is a crucial material for Laruelle for it offers a readymade model of cloning. The photographic image clones the Real insofar as it constructs an image that looks like the Real but is materially distinct from that which it pictures. Laruelle seizes on the immanent identity of the photograph or what Laruelle calls the "being-of-photo" or the "photo-as-photo."[40]

Laruelle's conceptualization of "being-photo of the photo" owes an acknowledged debt to the phenomenology of Edmund Husserl who set the course for the phenomenological project by articulating its central method of "bracketing" the question of reality so as to focus on describing experience as it appears. The phenomenological perspective grants "appearance" in its broadest sense an immanent reality. Phenomenology refuses to reduce appearances—images, fantasies, dreams, fears, hopes—to the status of the unreal and therefore the unimportant. It gives appearances the dignity of philosophical gravitas. Laruelle seeks to do the same for photographic images. Rather than test its significance against the presumed accessibility and stability of the Real, Laruelle treats the photographic image as an immanent identity in its own right. The image has the status of a clone, for like the clone of biotechnology, the photographic image is not simply a copy. The photographic image has its own identity quite apart from what it *resembles*. And it is this phenomenological autonomy of the *photo as photo* that Laruelle models his concept of non-philosophical cloning on. Laruelle's debt to the phenomenological tradition is clear in this passage from *The Concept of Non-Photography*:

> The whole lot of philosophical-type beliefs as to the real, as to knowledge, as to the image and as to representation and manifestation, must and can be eliminated so that we can describe, not the *being* of the photo but the *being-photo of the photo*. What is that nuance that separates the identity of photography, henceforth our guiding thread, from its being or its ontological interpretation?[41]

The identity of the *photo as photo* immanent to its own being provides a model for non-philosophical fiction. Non-philosophy in all its "fictional" forms aspires to the relative autonomy of the *photo as photo* as distinct from the what it pictures. Non-philosophical fiction (like photographic images) constitutes an autonomy and a fidelity to the Real. Non-philosophical fictions (like photographs) parallel the non-relationality of the Real. The photo's immanent identity as photo has no direct "relation" to the World it pictures even as it is determined by it. The photograph and the World parallel but do not "relate." "The photo is not a degradation of the World," writes Laruelle, "but a process which is 'parallel' to it. . . . We shall no longer say, then, that the photograph is a generalized simulacrum, a topology of the simulacrum."[42] The *photo as photo* parallels thought inasmuch as thought is neither entirely independent of the Real nor can it be entirely reduced to it. It is this "relative autonomy," this "nuance" between image-thought and the Real that non-philosophy under the sign of "non-photography" clones and reproduces within its strange syntax. Laruelle writes:

> To reprise—and radicalize—a distinction made by Husserl, we shall say that the object that is photographed or that *appears* "in" the photo . . . is wholly distinct from the photographic apparition or from the presentation of that object. . . . There is a "formal" being or a being-immanent of photographic apparition; it is, if you like, the photographic *phenomenon*, that which photography can manifest,

or more exactly, the manner, the "how" of its manifesting the World. This manner or this phenomenon—here is what radicalizes Husserl's distinction—distinguishes itself absolutely from the photographed object because it belongs to a wholly other sphere of reality.[43]

It is this thread of the "being of photo as photo" that links the case studies already mentioned. The case of Duchamp was (and is) also a case of photography, for it was as a photo that the fame/infamy of *Fountain* spread and still spreads. Troubling as it does the stability of the line between critique and creation, *Fountain* operates in the fissure between standard philosophical ideas and ideals of art— beauty, genius, individuality, aesthetic accomplishment—and an art of negation that problematizes both modern and postmodern signposts. There is an immanent truth-content internal to *Fountain* as a specific enactment and a generalized theory that challenges the universalizing tendencies of the disciplinary frames of standardized art historiography. *Fountain* calls out and creatively negates the authority of historiographical construction. *Fountain* asks: What is art *and* who decides? It parallels the non-philosophical challenge to the authority (and authoritarianism) of philosophy. Likewise, Julia Margaret Cameron's "soft focus" challenged the authority of the sharply focused image of standard, nineteenth-century photographic aesthetics. Finding a new focus, a new axiomatic, Cameron exposed sharp focus as an aesthetic norm or convention as Laruelle exposes the norms of standard philosophy.

Cameron and Duchamp both seized on the authority of standardized aesthetics and exposed it as a convention. Their work enacts an immanent truth-content that cannot be equated with, or reduced to, an imagined, external metric of "real" art or photography. And their accomplishments cannot be easily sandwiched into a convenient biography of excellence or exceptionalism. Duchamp's radically impersonal readymade works and Cameron's artfully staged artifices scramble any clear line of connection between them as persons and their practice. Contextual explanation (another favorite of art history) fares little better. Neither the norm of Victorian femininity nor the norm of modernist art historiography prove particularly useful guideposts for interpreting the work of Cameron or Duchamp respectively since in each case their work is precisely the exception to a rule. As Homi Bhabha notes:

> The attempt to connect a cultural context to an artist's consciousness—especially when the work's materials are foreign and unfamiliar—results in a sentimental exercise in establishing the artist's "authenticity" (as defined by the reigning criteria of the weekly review, or the scholarly journal, or recondite and recognizable icons of an "other" culture) rather than a critical engagement with the "authority" of the work.[44]

What is prescient for present purposes is Bhabha's concept of the "authority" of the work as a site of enunciation with the capacity to inverse the unilateral authority of philosophy and cultural frameworks. It is the aim of non-aesthetics to think in and through the "authority" of the *work* rather than the presumed authority and cultural value imposed and maintained by standard philosophical aesthetics or authorial-centric criticism. Non-aesthetics operates at an oblique angle to standard aesthetics. It operates not in the manner of critique or commentary but through a "scientific" process that seeks out the artwork's immanent "hypothesis." Laruelle writes:

> Two attitudes are excluded here: a "critical" and "aesthetic" commentary on the work and works, but also the very philosophy with which the artists themselves always accompany this work. . . . It is a question for us of seeking the theoretical effects or thought-effects that it produces, perhaps unknowingly, and in excess of what it knows. . . . We will treat their work, rather, as the equivalent of a *discovery*, an emergent novelty it falls to us precisely to produce the theory of, a theory which will also be something new in relation to "art criticism"—to pose it as *our* own object and thus to make the work of the artist resonate in our way, in the corresponding theory.[45]

Non-aesthetics rejects the spontaneous philosophy of the artists such as "artist statements" and instead considers the "practice" within the oeuvre as a single concept. Its aim is to trace (or de-scribe) the "theoretical effects" of this concept immanent in the artist's practice. This concept is to be treated as a "discovery" rather than a confirmation of the artist's statement, biography, or conventional philosophical aesthetics. The novelty of art practice is cloned into a parallel non-aesthetic theory or "fiction" thereby opening a line of fissure or flight with respect to "art criticism" in order to secure a relative autonomy for theory that parallels that of the art practice itself. Theory on this model does not directly correspond to the artwork, but "to the discovery to which it will have given rise."[46] Theory as such is not negated for art in non-aesthetics. Rather, the relation between art and theory is transformed intra-aesthetically. Laruelle's "discourse is by no means 'anti-theoretical,'" write Rocco Gangle and Julius Greve, "but works instead toward the construction of a theoretical apparatus that uses philosophy and related forms of thought in the same way a painter would make use of paintings."[47]

Laruelle's method is structured by an affirmation of the "reciprocal autonomy of art and theory," which, Laruelle concludes, "signifies that we are not the double of artists, that we also have a claim to 'creation,' and that inversely, artists are not the inverted doubles of aestheticians and that they, too, without being theorists, have a claim to the power of theoretical discovery."[48] Here the link with Adorno, Benjamin, Derrida, and other "creative" theorists is also clear. Like these critical-creative writers, Laruelle recognizes and deploys the aesthetics of aesthetics. But what makes non-aesthetic fiction unique is that it seeks to transform the aesthetics of aesthetics into a "science" of discovery. The aesthetic practice of non-aesthetics aims to treat a given art practice as a "hypothesis in the field of art."[49] Non-aesthetics aims at discovering this "hypothesis" more than proving or disproving it. Non-aesthetics divests from the standard critical objective to interpret the meaning of art—what it says—and instead seeks out its speculative moment—its *hypothesis.* The non-aesthetician responds to the discovery of this hypothesis with an "equivalent" or "clone" of "hypothetical speculation" or "fiction."

Fictional utopias

I want to draw out the utopian dimension of Laruelle's non-aesthetics by focusing on the work that "fiction" as a sign and strategy performs in his texts. Laruelle affirms Adorno's principled demand for thought to resist the given by creative composition. "Instead of reducing philosophy to categories," writes Adorno, "one would in a sense have to *compose* it first. Its course must be a ceaseless self-renewal, by its own strength as well as in a *friction* with whatever *standard* it may have."[50] "Composition" (*Komposition* in German) sits at the border of the literary, the philosophical, and the musical; a shared creative space that links the aesthetic and the theoretical dimensions of Adorno's philosophy and music. A philosophy of composition, Adorno writes, "is not expoundable."[51] The fact that much of philosophy "can be expounded," writes Adorno, "speaks against it."[52] No doubt the notorious difficulty of expounding Adorno's work could be seen in this light as something like an avant-gardist achievement. Commenting on Adorno's call for a philosophy of composition, Jonathan Culler writes that it

> is a literary way of conceiving philosophy—philosophy as a writing that achieves literary effects. This is not to imply that exposition of such texts is not necessary or desirable—only that such texts also require the kind of rhetorical readings and contextual analysis as acts, as performances.[53]

Culler is right up to a point. But from the non-philosophical vantage, the question is: What should "rhetorical readings" or "contextual analysis" produce? Should they further pry open the space of composition to find (force) meaning? The non-standard condition of criticism—or in Adorno's slightly different sense, that "friction" with "standard" philosophical criticism—must resist the desire to give voice to *expounding* meaning in the name of *expanding* compositional space. The space of philosophical composition is, as Culler rightly notes, a "performance." I want to conclude this chapter by drawing out the fictional and the performative dimensions of non-philosophy generally and non-aesthetics specifically. My aim here is to specify the utopian dimension of the fictional and the performative in Laruelle's work.

In *Philosophy and Non-Philosophy*, Laruelle writes: "Fiction is a marginal and ambitious figure of the philosophical scene."[54] Fiction is "marginal" for philosophy is still centered by the practice of expounding, but fiction is also for this very reason "ambitious" for it challenges this very centrality from the periphery. This operation from the margins creates "friction" with the "central" aims of standard philosophy. From the margins, the center is de-scribed, un-done, or reframed in novel ways that open spaces that are imaginary and utopic, creating a virtual map of what philosophy might become in the absence of its authoritarian authority. The status of fiction, writes Laruelle, "has suffered under the 'real.' . . . Fiction's life is conflated with its struggles to exist and receive a concept."[55] To conceptualize fiction in the standard philosophical sense means contrasting it against presumed knowledge of the Real. But this measure by which philosophy frames fiction is itself a fiction of philosophy according to Laruelle. The fictions of non-philosophy, by contrast, aim to render material the fiction of any philosophical concept of the Real. But as for standard philosophy, it only "tolerates fiction on condition of . . . deciding on its essence."[56]

Fiction, for Laruelle, has for too long been subject to philosophy's presupposed sufficiency to decide its status via a judgment on its bearing on the Real. But fiction is neither real nor unreal, neither false nor true: it is of an entirely different order of statement-making. There is something provisionally utopic about fiction in its power to exile itself from the realm of the Real ruled by philosophy; indeed, fiction can operate as a resistance to the Real. Fiction works through a "displacement of the angle of vision," in Benjamin's poignant phrase.[57] Fiction can show us how things are, but also how they might be. Here, again, Adorno turns out to be a strange bedfellow. In the final entry of *Minima Moralia*, he writes:

> The only philosophy which can be responsibly practiced in the face of despair is the attempt to contemplate all things as they would present themselves from the standpoint of redemption. Knowledge has no light but that shed on the world by redemption: all else is reconstruction, mere technique. Perspectives must be fashioned that displace and estrange the world, reveal it to be, with its rifts and crevices, as indigent and distorted as it will one day appear in the messianic light.[58]

Philosophy in a time of terror has to be something more than an empirical "double of the world."[59] The philosopher is ethically compelled to fashion perspectives that will "displace" and "estrange" the given world. These fashioned perspectives must approximate an image of the world as it will appear in a "messianic light," from the standpoint of "redemption," which, paradoxically, is to see it *as it is* with all its "rifts and crevices." The messianic perspective is not, on my reading, the world seen through rose-colored glasses; it is the world seen in the light of the distortions and rifts that lie beneath the world's paper-thin facade of administered normality. To philosophize in a messianic light is to see the world put on its "true Surrealist face" in Benjamin's words.[60] The messianic perspective is one of redemptive judgment and justice. It will see the cruelty of the world—it will see the face of the victim—who will no longer appear in the pale light of indifference and banality.[61] Messianic light is the light of justice done and seen; for *justice must not only be done; it must be seen to be done.*

Adorno's art of fashioning perspectives parallels Laruelle's sense of non-philosophy as a fabricating or fictionalizing process, opening and revealing spaces which *appear* outside the horizon of the Real while remaining immanently conditioned by it. For the fictionalized, fashioned, imagined, messianic perspective is in the last instance "utterly impossible," writes Adorno, "because it presupposes a standpoint removed" by a "hair's breadth from the scope of existence."[62] The fabricated or fashioned perspectives of fiction enable non-philosophy to at once look beyond the Real as it appears in philosophy while reflecting on the conditions of pain and inhumanity that immanently conditions that "from which it seeks to escape."[63] The art of fashioning perspectives—an art of philosophical fiction or "philo-fiction," in Laruelle's words—transposes the problematic of aesthetics from art to philosophy in order to wrest open the fictive and utopic possibilities that attend art's exilic trajectory launched first by Plato.

Non-aesthetics introjects aesthetics into the syntax of philosophical "composition" to exile philosophy from its seat of sovereign power. The "non" of non-philosophy generally, and non-aesthetics specifically, marks an exilic estrangement of standard philosophy and standard aesthetics from their power. The "non" is neither simply negation nor is it philosophy's radical other. Non-aesthetics does not seek "a theory of art that is other than philosophical," writes Laruelle, "since all theory would, in any case, include a philosophical aspect."[64] Rather than elaborating a set of criteria for aesthetic judgment, non-aesthetics catalyzes an itinerary of speculation. "Can aesthetics become a second power of art itself, can art engender or determine its own aesthetics instead of suffering" whatever is "philosophically imposed on it?"[65]

Photography again offers Laruelle a readymade model. Photo-fiction is "a model for philo-fiction," which is "no longer Platonic" for it does not presuppose a correspondence to the "truth" of art any more than a photographic image presupposes a correspondence to the truth of the visible. Photo-fiction is neither "photographical [n]or . . . philosophical," writes Laruelle, instead we "must compare it with the terms of art-fiction and philo-fiction as well as that of science fiction. Photo-fiction is a *genre*."[66] In the chapters to follow, we will explore these genres of non-philosophical writing in more depth. But for present purposes, I want to focus on the fictive element that unites them as well as their implications for utopian imagining.

Alexander R. Galloway conceptualizes the genres of non-philosophy as variations on what he calls Laruelle's "process[es] of non-standardization."[67] "Fiction means performance, invention, creativity, artifice, construction; for example, thought is fictive because it fabricates (although only in an immanent and real sense)."[68] Galloway continues:

> *Fiction* might seem like a strange word choice for someone wishing to depart from the endless alternations of representation, yet Laruelle devises a type of fiction that is nonexpressive and nonrepresentational. Laruelle's fiction is purely immanent to itself. It is neither a fictionalized version of something else, nor does it try to fabricate a fictitious world or narrative based on real or fantastical events.[69]

Non-philosophical fiction is neither representational nor fantastical nor expressive; all these are modes of correspondence to an externality. Laruelle's idea (and ideal for it may well be impossible) is to cleave out a form of philosophical fiction that is almost entirely self-referential. There is a strain of modernist yearning here: the aesthetic yearning for radical autonomy from representationalism. "Laruelle's utopia is a non-world," writes Galloway, "yet a non-world entirely rooted in the present. Laruelle's non-world is, in fact, entirely real."[70] Like Adorno's "messianic light," the non-philosophical yearning for a non-world—utopic place—is conditioned by the present and its constraints. Non-aesthetics carves out a place for theory alongside art just as non-philosophy parallels the Real, but in both cases, the Real is held to be determinant in the last instance. Laruelle's "utopian real is a *parallelism*," concludes Galloway.[71]

The parallelism of non-aesthetics to art is secured through a "matrix" that combines fictive elements extrapolated from philosophical, literary, and scientific language. The matrix combines these elements, but it strips them of their representationalist functions. "I propose to consider every art form," writes Laruelle, "no longer in terms of descriptive or theoretical or foundational historical perspectives."[72] Such a radical break with the mimeticism of the phenomenology of art, art criticism, and art history requires that one fabricate or "construct non-aesthetic scenarios or duals, scenes, characters, or postures that are both conceptual and artistic based on the formal model of a matrix."[73] Ontologies of art are not countenanced for the matrix itself provides Laruelle with an ontological form. What is essential to the question of the essence of art for non-philosophy is the essentiality of art's modes of construction as fabrication, fictionalization, or performance. Laruelle writes:

> We will not start from . . . [the] question, we will not ask *what is art?* . . . A matrix is a mathematical mode of organization and a presentation of the data of a problem when there are at least two heterogeneous, conceptual, and artistic data that are linked in what we will call a matrixial manner.[74]

The multiplicity of ways in which artistic, philosophical, and scientific material can be matrixed—the various scenarios that can be plotted—correspond "by their inventive and constructive aspects" to "veritable theoretical 'installations.'"[75] The non-aesthetic matrix superposes aesthetic and philosophical raw materials in the manner of installation art: a bricolage of decontextualized and recontextualized raw materials that are matrixed (but not mixed) together. The matrixial mode of non-aesthetics, writes Laruelle, is "thought itself striving to be an art . . .

an art of thought rather than thought about art."[76] This practice "is not a meta-art," continues Laruelle, "but a non-aesthetic art, of a non-standard aesthetics. . . . Not a conceptual art, but a concept modeled by . . . art, a generic extension of art."[77] Here the term "extension" should itself be extended in the direction of something more like "supplement." For non-aesthetics does not simply or solely *extend* the dimension of art or that of philosophy; it transforms the fabric of the relation internally through a supplementary co-imbrication of art and philosophy in the "matrix" of non-philosophy.

Matrixial thought, in my view, parallels the theoretical figure of "Third Space" as articulated in the work of Homi Bhabha. Conceptualizing his particular and profoundly inventive style of postcolonial theorizing, Bhabha coins "Third Space" to mark contact zones where theoretical, cultural, historical, and/or psychic antagonisms and affiliations are hybridized through ambivalent processes of junction and disjunction. In his landmark essay, "The Commitment to Theory," Bhabha writes:

> The pact of interpretation is never simply an act of communication between the I and the You designated in the statement. The production of meaning requires that these two places be mobilized in the passage through a Third Space, which represents both the general conditions of language and the specific implications of the utterance in a performative and institutional strategy of which it cannot "in itself" be conscious.[78]

The reinterpretation of philosophical aesthetics through the practice and performance of non-aesthetics opens a Third Space, in Bhabha's sense, that rearticulates the conscious and unconscious relations between the "specific utterance" of the artwork and the "institutional strategy" by which this specificity is interpreted. Non-aesthetics as matrix or Third Space provisionally marks a "site of enunciation" at which the general or generic conditions of language cross the untranslatable specificities of the artwork.[79]

The matrix or Third Space of non-aesthetics creates a fiction of art and philosophy that cannot in the last instance be reduced to either. "When non-philosophy engages with art," writes Anthony Paul Smith, "it cannot simply be through writing a gallery catalogue, but must find a way to turn itself into a kind of artistic practice by using artistic materials."[80] Non-aesthetics opens a Third Space beyond the binary of art/theory and forces to the fore the heterogeneous and historical conditions that frame the relationship between these two highly contested terms, "art" and "theory."

In the dizzying contact zone of Third Space, in the midst of its matrixial mechanics, the aesthetics of art and the aesthetics of thought are "superposed." The superposed enunciative conditions of art and philosophy cross to "perform the art of thought rather than produce a thought about art."[81] The space of superposition, the matrixial re-articulation of art and philosophy, the passage through the Third Space—in the final analysis, what is at stake is an effort to reimagine utopian thought as the possibility of the impossible within the strictures and the structures of the Real. Rather than the utopian hope that art will change the World as figured by philosophy, Laruelle evokes the potential for *an art of non-philosophy* that will de-substantialize the gravitas of the philosophical image of the World. His fictions aim at nothing less than a radical "counter-creation to that of the world."[82] Philo-fiction—the art of thought—is "a force of insurrection that disempowers the world and operates without concern for its parameters."[83]

3

The Aesthetics and Ethics of Non-Philosophy

This chapter further explores the matrixial mechanics of Laruelle's work. We will examine in more depth how Laruelle matrices the "languages" of photography, philosophy, and especially quantum physics, in order to derive and develop a measure of novelty and a degree of autonomy for the practice of theorizing art. We will examine the "quantic" (Laruelle's term) dimension of non-aesthetics by turning first to an exploration of Michael Frayn's Tony Award–winning play, *Copenhagen*. The play is based on an actual but little understood event—Werner Heisenberg's mysterious trip to Copenhagen in 1941 to see his mentor, Niels Bohr. We will explore this play from the perspective of what Frayn calls "quantum ethics" before turning back to Laruelle to see how he develops a quantum perspective for the practice of non-aesthetics. Of central concern will be the "superposition" of ethics and aesthetics. We will then take a closer look at the meaning of theoretical practice in non-philosophy through a study of the aesthetic and ethico-political stakes of non-philosophy via an examination of Laruelle's response to Marxism. This, in turn, will lead finally to a discussion of Laruelle's radical ethics of the human.

Quantum ethics

Toward the close of Act II of Michael Frayn's *Copenhagen*, Bohr says: "Heisenberg, I have to say—if people are to be measured strictly in terms of observable quantities . . ."; Heisenberg finishes his sentence: "Then we should need a strange new quantum ethics."[1] What came to be called the Copenhagen Interpretation of quantum physics was the work of many eminent scientists, but at its heart was the work of Niels Bohr and Werner Heisenberg. The counterintuitive results of landmark experiments—most famously the "double-slit" experiment—revealed that the world of atomic particles does not conform to the macroscopic or "classical" worldview established by Newton. The behavior of billiard balls, planets, apples, and the like, operate according to clearly defined causal laws of predictability. But Bohr and Heisenberg's picture of the quantum world depicted a topos of uncertainty and probability. The double-slit experiment had shown that even single particles appear on occasion to follow a trajectory from the particle emitter through *both* slits, interfering with itself, creating a wave-like pattern, the signature of interference, on the sensor. The strange "non-locality" of the quantum particle—its potential to be indeterminately in more than one location simultaneously—came to be called "superposition." And the observed particle-like and wave-like structures of atomic phenomena were to lead Bohr to advance the Complementarity Principle that states that particle-like and wave-like descriptions of atomic phenomena are equally valid. Arguably the most far-reaching philosophical consequence of the Copenhagen Interpretation, however, was Heisenberg's Uncertainty Principle for which he was awarded the Nobel Prize. Put very simply, the Uncertainty Principle states that it is impossible to know with absolute certainty the position and momentum of a particle. The more you know about one, the less you know about the other.

The Copenhagen Interpretation was far from intuitive even for Bohr and Heisenberg. The phenomenology of quantum behavior, according to the Copenhagen Interpretation, defeats common sense. It is a world in which things in a sense can occupy more than one location at a time; where things can be wave-like or particle-like; where full knowledge of a system is structurally impossible; and where commonsense causal relations cannot be applied innocently. But what is also strange is that observation never shows a particle in a mixed state or in more than one location. Observation seems to resolve the indeterminacy in atomic systems. What is called the "observer-effect" cannot be discounted for the observer—the scientist and/or the instruments of observation—are also atomic systems and these have a non-trivial effect on that which they observe. This means that there is a fundamental barrier between observation and observed. There is no way to study atomic behavior without changing it. The philosophical consequences of what Bohr called the "quantum postulate" doubled and redoubled in an epistemological chain reaction: locality, states, causation, consciousness, free-will, aesthetics, ethics. The classical worldview and its epistemology was impossible to square with the quantum postulate.

Frayn's play centers on an actual historical event. In 1941, Heisenberg, who at the time held the chair in physics at Leipzig University, travelled at great risk to Copenhagen to see his former mentor, Niels Bohr. Heisenberg was given permission to travel by the Nazi government. He travelled from Berlin to Copenhagen by train. But he was conspicuously followed by Nazi intelligence. What he said, where he went, and what he did were closely observed. Any perceived misstep would have meant arrest at least. He was tolerated by the Nazis on account of his professional standing (and because he was not Jewish). But his commitment to the physics of Einstein—denounced as "Jewish physics" by the Nazis—made him a figure of suspicion. By 1941 many of Germany's eminent physicists had fled or been captured. Heisenberg's decision to stay was at the time (and still is) seen as a case of opportunism at best. His decision to travel to Occupied Denmark also put Bohr and his wife Margrethe at considerable risk. The Bohrs had reason to believe that they were already under surveillance and that their beautiful home at Carlsberg, given in honor of Niels Bohr winning the Nobel Prize in 1922, had been bugged.

What everyone concerned wanted to know was why? What was the purpose of the trip? Even Bohr and Heisenberg never could agree precisely on what the reason had been nor what exactly had been said at the meeting. All that is certain is that this fateful encounter in Copenhagen in 1941 marked the end of twenty years of close friendship between the two. Heisenberg returned one last time to Copenhagen after the war in 1947. This time he was followed by British intelligence. On this second trip, Heisenberg sought a rapprochement with Bohr and to see if they could agree on what happened. Heisenberg noted in his memoirs that the attempt failed for "we both came to feel that it would be better to stop disturbing the spirits of the past."[2] This presented Frayn with his point of departure. Frayn notes:

> This is where my play departs from the historical record by supposing that . . . when everyone involved had become spirits of the past themselves, they argued the question out . . . just as they had so many times when they were alive with the intractable difficulties presented by the internal workings of the atom.[3]

Frayn consulted numerous biographies, published accounts, and other assorted archival traces and historical reconstructions. Yet he still feels "acutely how over-simplified my version [of the history of quantum physics] is."[4] But it must be said that the history of quantum physics is difficult because it is a history that superposes science, philosophy, ethics, and even aesthetics (as evidenced in the driving search for elegant theories). Frayn notes: "Max Born described the real story [of quantum physics] as not so much 'a straight staircase upwards, but a tangle of interconnected alleys,' and I found it impossible to follow these in any detail (even where I can begin to understand them)."[5]

Frayn's research into the "tangled alleys" of quantum physics led him into labyrinthine histories and inscrutably difficult epistemologies. The particulars of the history, the subject, and the encounter in Copenhagen between Bohr and Heisenberg involved Frayn in interminable and unresolvable uncertainties of science, history, and the "internal workings" of Bohr, Heisenberg, Margrethe, their relationships with one another, the war, Nazism, Los Alamos, Hiroshima, Nagasaki. The uncertain causal chains of action and reaction branched out before Frayn as he tried to observe and follow its leads. Writing led him inexorably into the historical, epistemological, and literary uncertainties of a world precariously positioned on the pivot between past and present, science and literature, fact and fiction.

How to write this? How to give voice to a voiceless history, but one so replete with resounding consequences? How to write through the blanks in the historical record and the gaps in understanding? For Frayn, it was at once a question of ethics and aesthetics. How to give form to the uncertainties of the historical and epistemological record? Frayn looked to Thucydides for guidance. The ancient historian noted in his *History of the Peloponnesian War* that though he had scrupulously sought to avoid any hint of "storytelling" on the grounds that history is not a story, he found that when it came to reciting speeches: "I have found it impossible to remember the exact wording. Hence I have made each orator speak as, in my opinion, he would have done in the circumstances, but keeping as close to the train of thought that guided his actual speech."[6] Frayn's remarkable insight on this point is worth quoting at length.

> Thucydides was trying to give an account of speeches that had actually been made, many of which he had himself heard. Some of the dialogue in my play represents speeches that must have been made in one form or another; some of its speeches were certainly never made at all. I hope, though, that in some sense it respects the Thucydidean principle, and that speeches (and indeed actions) follow in so far as possible the original protagonists' train of thought. But how far is it possible to know what the train of thought was? This is where I have departed from the established historical record—from any possible historical record. The great challenge facing the storyteller and the historian alike is to get inside people's heads, to stand where they stood and see the world as they saw it, to make some informed estimate of their motives and intentions—and this is precisely where recorded and recordable history cannot reach. Even when all the external evidence has been mastered, the only way into the protagonists' heads is through the imagination. This is indeed the substance of the play.[7]

The archive of "recorded and recordable history" tells us little to nothing about individual motives. Even when and where motives appear in the historical transcript, they must be read with the requisite suspicion. Intentions and motives often emerge in *media res* in the very acts themselves. "Decisions make themselves," as Heisenberg says to Bohr at one point in the play.[8] Frayn's play confronts the difficult question of intentionality and motivation—those psychological blanks within recorded and recordable history.

The structure of Frayn's play parallels a particle experiment. Bohr, Heisenberg, and Margrethe—now ghosts—run through iteration after iteration of the meeting in Copenhagen in 1941 trying to ascertain what Heisenberg's motives were for making the risky trip. But each time, with each new iteration of the experiment, the protagonists observe some other phenomena that open new historical and ethical questions. There are overlaps between the iterations, but the overlapping observations are made by different characters at different times. No character has a singular and cohesive account or a stable matrix of observed quantities. Despite their best intentions to "add up the arguments . . . in a reasonably scientific way," as Bohr says, they fail to reconstruct and finally understand the event as it happened in 1941.[9] Each new iteration creates new intentions and motives: the will to understand what happened in 1941 is entirely different than the intentions and motives that framed the trip in the first instance. They reconstruct the event, but each time the intentions and motives that conditioned the 1941 encounter grow only more obscure. "No one understands my trip to Copenhagen," confesses Heisenberg.[10] "Time and time again," he continues, "I've explained it. To Bohr himself, and Margrethe. To interrogators and intelligence officers, to journalists and historians. The more I have explained, the deeper the uncertainty has become."[11] With each iteration, the "uncertainty" increases. Was it to reconnect with an old friend? Was it to see if Bohr knew anything about the Allied bomb program? Was it to tell Bohr that Allied and Axis scientists should work together to stop such a program? Having found each of these explanations insufficient, they resolve to try again.

Bohr: So, Heisenberg, why did you come?
Heisenberg: Why did I come?
Bohr: Tell us once again. Another draft of the paper. And this time we shall get it right. This time we will understand.
Margrethe: Maybe you'll even understand yourself.[12]

But this draft also fails to provide the certainty they seek. With each new draft of the paper, the uncertainty of what happened, and the evidence that this may never be known, grows skyward. The three have spent their lives since 1941 trying to "lay their hands" on the truth only to discover that everything depends on knowing for sure what was in their heads or hearts that day in Copenhagen.

> **Bohr**: Before we can lay our hands on anything, our life's over.
> **Heisenberg**: Before we can glimpse who or what we are, we're gone and laid to dust.
> **Bohr**: Settled among all the dust we raised.[13]

Despite their continually frustrated attempts to know what happened and to know themselves, they press on to yet more drafts. What are they forging? Inchoately and unconsciously they are seeking a theory of "quantum ethics" in order to answer those moral dilemmas that mark their lives, like all lives, and that resist easy partition into good and bad.

> **Heisenberg**: Why did I come to Copenhagen? Yes, why did I come?
> **Bohr**: One more draft, yes? One final draft!
> **Heisenberg**: And once again I crunch over the familiar gravel to the Bohrs' front door, and tug at the familiar bell-pull. Why have I come? I know perfectly well. Know so well that I've no need to ask myself. Until once again the heavy door opens.
> **Bohr**: He stands on the doorstep blinking in the sudden flood of light from the house. Until this instant his thoughts have been everywhere and nowhere, like unobserved particles, through all the slits in the diffraction grating simultaneously. Now they have to be observed and specified.
> **Heisenberg**: And at once the clear purposes inside my head lose all definite shape. The light falls on them and they scatter.
> **Bohr**: My dear Heisenberg!
> **Heisenberg**: My dear Bohr!
> **Bohr**: Come in, come in . . .
> **Heisenberg**: How difficult it is to see even what's in front of one's eyes. All we possess is the present, and the present endlessly dissolves into the past. Bohr has gone even as I turn to see Margrethe.[14]

Heisenberg knows "perfectly well" why he has come to Copenhagen *until* the "door opens." At that moment, his intentions and motives "scatter." At the moment when intentions and motives must be observed, accounted, and "specified," then "the clear purposes inside my head lose all definite shape." New intentions and new motives begin to make themselves. Prior intentions and motives— never fully articulated—now scatter in the light from the house and the sight of Bohr. And in turning to Margrethe, these new intentions, in turn, give way to yet newer ones. Decisions make themselves. All that remains amid the ruins of incomplete drafts, unspecified intentions, unrecordable histories is an event in Copenhagen in 1941. The wayward path of forking decisions and the chain of uncertainties that just possibly disallowed a Nazi bomb will have only been by virtue of "some event that will never be located or defined," Heisenberg concludes. "By that final core of uncertainty at the heart of things."[15]

Frayn ingeniously clones the mechanics of quantum interactions into the mechanics of human relations. What Laruelle might call the "generic" structure of quantum uncertainty provides Frayn with an ethical measure—a "quantum ethics"—to work through a set of difficult concerns: the politics of friendship, ethical responsibility, the precarity of memory, the contingencies of history. Frayn's work neither absolves nor aggrandizes. The Second World War is represented at the micrological scale of human intimacies fraught with the perplexities of what Homi Bhabha might call "intimate alterity." Distances open up between the characters in *Copenhagen* and within themselves that are estranging and defamiliarizing precisely because they open from within the interstices of intimacy. They are strangers to themselves and to each other in the very precise sense that Anthony Paul Smith has given the term. "What makes someone a stranger," writes Smith, "is not a totally unrecognizable nature, but a commonality that yet does not fit into one's own framework for making sense of a certain field of experience."[16] The strangeness of estrangement belies an intimacy. To become estranged is to experience what Walter Benjamin in a certain sense meant by the "aura"—"a distance no matter how close."[17]

Frayn is not a physicist. His interest in the history of physics lies in the all-too-human story of uncertain relations and ethical quandaries that produced a meeting in Copenhagen in 1941; and possibly, just possibly, a chain of reactions from Bohr's home to Los Alamos, to Hiroshima and Nagasaki, and to recriminations, recusals, and regrets by all involved ever since that fateful day in 1941. But this chain, this narrative arc, the surety and certainty of this history, is undercut by a deep and abiding "uncertainty at the heart of things." We cannot know for sure what happened in 1941 in Copenhagen nor what, if any, effect this had on history. And yet, and this is key, Frayn's "quantum ethics" demands that we try and take the measure of responsibility while recognizing the uncertainty that necessarily attends that effort. Draft after draft will have to be made. Each time the uncertainty will grow. But each time we wrest from history some other vantage that just might possibly provide the ethical resources we need to survive our histories.

Quantic fiction

Frayn's play is situated on the borders between aesthetics, science, and ethics. The ethical quandaries of historical responsibility and historical uncertainty find their aesthetic form in a set of quantum metaphors: chain reactions, collisions, recoils, diffractions, uncertainty. This nexus is also decisive for Laruelle's "quantic" philo-fictions.

The popularity of quantum physics has engendered a whole host of commodified mysticisms that appropriate the language and imagery of quantum physics to advance dubious philosophies and commercialized spiritualities. Laruelle does not exactly distinguish himself from the crowded stage of new-age philosophers with comments like this.

Another form of knowledge is necessary, at once scientific and of some philosophical kind, one without reflection but through superposition of the quantum and philosophy. Without this no one can understand more clearly this formula: philo-fiction, indeed even theo-fiction, is a science-fiction with possibly its classical technology augmented with that of philosophy, but the sense of which is human or the vector that is "messianic."[18]

The quasi-mystical and rhetorical force that produces "another knowledge" or what Laruelle earlier calls "gnosis" superposed with that of "the quantum" and the "messianic" ought to raise eyebrows. As Keith Tilford notes, Laruelle's "quasi-mysticism" places "all of his trust in the metaphorical power of quantum superposition, which conditions and safeguards them against contradiction on the very basis of its being a metaphor."[19] The power of metaphor is all that keeps the "quasi" intact and prevents Laruelle's work from falling into the worst species of new-age thought and pseudo-science. Metaphor is a powerful "surface of conversion" in Rancière's words for it transcodes and transposes the terms of one discourse into those of another. It is a power that allows thought to move from one locale to another while never settling into or identifying with a given terrain. Metaphor is a *way* of thinking and speaking that enables one to ironically identify with what is signified from a point of distance and disidentification under the sign of "metaphor" or "metaphorically speaking." But we could just as easily call this power of metaphor "fiction" or more generically "literature."

Laruelle's messianic dimension here is comparable to Adorno's "messianic light." Neither figuration need be taken in anything more than a this-world way. Whereas Adorno sought a measure of ethical rectitude in philosophical "composition" to steer clear of the trap of doubling the world in thought, Laruelle seeks "another knowledge" not *beyond* but *irreducible* to science or philosophy. "Superposition," in non-philosophical terms, is a human fabrication or fictionalization oriented by an immanent messianic vector that "redeems" science and philosophy by respecting their autonomy while cloning the terms of each into an aesthetics and an ethics for thinking differently in order to produce "another knowledge."

Non-philosophy's superposed fiction of quantum physics and philosophy makes no claims about atomic phenomena nor does it render a Philosophical Decision of any kind. What it accomplishes is what Laruelle calls "vision-force" or "vision-in-One," a way of envisioning or thinking the Real as One as decisive in the last instance, without trying this vision before the tribunal of philosophy. This vision has the *form*, but not the *content*, of a gnostic or mystical vision. The mystic's vision is neither true nor false but is fictive for it envisions "another knowledge" that cannot be assimilated by the frameworks of philosophical argument or scientific proof. This is at once the freedom and the risk of non-philosophy; a risk and a freedom not unlike that of literature and art. "Running throughout non-philosophy," notes Smith, "is a kind of aesthetic vision as he [Laruelle] attempts to bring together various forms of thinking, but without endeavoring to provide the usual philosophical arguments" or scientific proofs.[20]

Working with the raw materials of philosophy, science, photography, theology, and art, Laruelle elaborates cloned versions of non-philosophy: philo-fiction, science fiction, photo-fiction, theo-fiction, and art-fiction. The "proliferation of various kinds of fictions" within non-philosophy "can be seen as a proliferation of various kinds of knowledges," notes Smith, "not producing knowledge separate from those practices, but understanding those practices as themselves forms of knowledge."[21] The various forms of non-philosophical fiction seek out the knowledge immanent to science, art, photography, and theology without extracting and philosophically transcoding that knowledge into a philosophical subject, discipline, or object of study. But is this possible? How can one treat art, science, photography, and other practices as knowledge without making a philosophical claim about (on) them? Michael Frayn's *Copenhagen* is one answer.

Copenhagen does not make any scientific claims about quantum physics nor does it make any claims about the Real of the historical event of Bohr and Heisenberg's fateful meeting in 1941. It treats these as raw materials for the composition of an "aesthetic vision" through which the play frames an ethical problematic. Science and history are quite what they were before, but something new emerges from within the matrix of Frayn's non-scientific and non-historical use of science and history that accedes to visibility without occluding the epistemological and historical opacities that still mark the event. The quantum becomes a "quantic" structure—a point of internal conversion—that iteratively converts the aesthetic into the ethical and back again ceaselessly.

Smith's observation that Laruelle's work converts art and science into an "aesthetic vision" is half-right, for this very point of conversion is also an ethical practice. To convert science and art into an aesthetic vision is a *choice* to make or fabricate this very vision. In this choice, in this practice, or in this performance of non-philosophy, Laruelle enacts what philosophy *ought* to become: free and "autonomous" as art and science. The aesthetic vision is also an ethical vantage that imagines a utopic condition of (and for) thought in which thought recomposes itself in a "messianic light" no longer under the authoritarian weight of standard philosophy. Frayn's play enacts a conversion from quantum science to an ethically bounded quantum aesthetics; Laruelle's fiction enacts a conversion of art and science into an iterative practice of the ethics and aesthetics of thought. As Laruelle notes in *Photo-Fiction*:

> To think "aesthetics" in the form of scenarios, quantically conjugating a variety of arts and philosophies, would enrich and liberate possible productive forces and would justify the existence of art not as thought, as was talked about with post-modernists, but a veritable thought-art. . . . In any case, one must not only "decompartmentalize" disciplinary domains (and the arts spontaneously agree), but find positive and systematic reasons that impose this decompartmentalization and which are not content to merely follow it. We must not only conjugate these domains instead of blending them together, but to know how to superpose them.[22]

Note the ethical demands from the above passage. To think aesthetics from the non-standard perspective of "quantically" conjugated "scenarios" drawn from a host of scientific and artistic practices requires that one not only "decompartmentalize" the disciplinary divisions between practices—which has been underway in the arts since the "postmodern" turn—but also, and importantly, to locate "positive and systematic reasons" that "impose this decompartmentalization." Let us return to Rauschenberg's *Reservoir* (Figure 2) for a moment to consider this in more detail.

It was Leo Steinberg who first used the term "postmodern" to describe the work of Robert Rauschenberg. Steinberg argued that Rauschenberg's juxtaposed images and materials broke the function and format of the Greenbergian "surface" of modernist painting and reconstructed it as a "flatbed" surface like the surface of a flatbed truck—a ground of accretion as against the idealized flat surface; the supposedly pure ground-zero prescribed by the modernist ontology of painting.[23] The move from flatness (Greenberg) to "flatbed" (Steinberg) marks an important shift in what Rancière, as we saw, identifies as the conversionary "surface" of philosophical aesthetics that transcodes the seeable into the sayable. The flatbed surfaces of postmodernity that Steinberg identified in Rauschenberg's work (and elsewhere) organized a pattern of postmodern theorizing that prized the erosion of disciplinary domains. Laruelle's "decompartmentalization" of science and art, and the matrixial mechanics by which he quantically conjugates these into fictions, parallels Rauschenberg's "postmodern" flatbed aesthetics. The two appear on this point to "spontaneously agree." But the limit of this spontaneous agreement is that it is forged on the basis of an already philosophically decided set of criteria—the postmodern—which secures the agreement and "allows" philosophy to be like art and vice versa. The point, for Laruelle, is to go beyond this agreement that art is a form of thought to accede to a "thought-art," a quantic conjugation that is not mediated by philosophy's decision as to what art thinks or how.

Non-aesthetics goes beyond the patronizing gesture of recognizing the intellectual value and significance of art. It challenges itself to seek out the philosophical "discovery" of the work itself. To return to the example of Rauschenberg, non-aesthetics would have to not merely recognize and "follow" its ethic of "decompartmentalization" but should also discover "systematic reasons" for this decompartmentalization. There are reasons why Rauschenberg's work acceded to an aesthetic of decompartmentalization. Overdetermined and palimpsestitical as these reasons are, there are reasons. The point for non-aesthetics is then to clone this discovery and materialize it in the matrix of its expository frame. We pass then through the nexus of the aesthetic and the ethical in posing the question: What forms can the quantically conjugated fictions or scenarios of non-philosophy take and why should a certain form be imposed? The what and the why—the structuring form (aesthetics) and the "systematic reasons" (ethics) for non-philosophy must be realized in material form in the matrices and syntaxes of its fiction. Let us further examine this in light of Laruelle's practice of photo-fiction.

Photo-fiction is given its most extensive treatment in *The Concept of Non-Photography* and *Photo-Fiction*. I will draw on both texts in order to bring into focus the ethical dimension of Laruelle's non-aesthetics. Photo-fiction is strategically situated at the border of photography and quantum physics. The historical course of quantum physics from its earliest days through the Copenhagen Interpretation into the present has been profoundly marked and shaped by questions concerning the behavior of particles of light or "photons."[24] And, as Arkady Plotnitsky points out, photography was central to the study of photons early on. Experimenters would fire photons at photosensitized sheets to capture the barest trace of their existence. Photography, literally "light-writing," and research into the strange behavior of photons were historically and materially imbricated.

Photo-fiction likewise matrixes or quantically conjugates photonic phenomena and the writing or tracing of light in the practice of photography. Photography itself, it should be noted, was historically a conjugation of art and science. At its advent in the mid-nineteenth century, photography was torn between those who saw it as a scientific instrument and those, like Cameron, who saw it as a medium for artistic expression. This split resounded through nearly a century of critical writing that pitted objectivist and subjectivist views of photography against one another.

Photo-fiction is likewise in a superposed state, a state of non-locality, with respect to the domains of art and philosophy as traditionally defined. Photo-fiction occupies an intermediary and indeterminate location between the actuality of quantum physics and photography. But, perhaps the most fitting metaphor for photo-fiction is that of "model." As the philosopher of science, Margaret Morrison notes, the model "is able to mediate between theory and the world and intervene in both domains."[25] The model frequently takes the form of an idealized representation, a theoretical fiction of sorts, and yet "fictional models can still deliver scientifically and philosophically valuable information."[26] Photo-fiction (and its related practices) might be best understood as a model or even a process of modeling in which the artistic and scientific domains are cloned into an aesthetical and ethical model or matrix. This is clear in the following passage from *Photo-Fiction*: "This photo-fictional theoretical apparatus will be an aesthetic impossibility, a non-aestheticizable or non-philosophizable impossibility, and it is as such that it will realize a non-aesthetics of the photo."[27] Here we have to take "photo" in a superposed sense. "Photo" here means *both* the photograph and its photonic correlate in quantum physics. The "photo-fictional theoretical apparatus" is a model or matrix that superposes the theoretical and empirical dimensions of photography (its material and discourse) to produce an "art-thought" that is neither solely theoretical nor solely philosophical or scientific, but is rather a hypothetical fiction like Frayn's *Copenhagen*, which is irreducible to aesthetics or science. This matrixial model parallels the constitution of photography as an art and a science of light. Laruelle continues:

> This photo-fictional apparatus is probably not made for taking pictures to put into albums or the more modern methods of viewing photos, it is made only for generating fictions that are like "theoretical captions" that eventually accompany the photos. Let us invert the Platonic relation of Ideas to objects that copy them.[28]

Laruelle's key point here, putting aside his irony, is that photo-fictions "invert" the "Platonic relation of Ideas to object." Whereas Plato held that the Idea was the genesis of the object, Laruelle de-schematizes the relationship altogether. Ideas and objects occupy no predetermined hierarchical structure. They asymmetrically parallel one another. The philosopher-king of Plato—the authority of (and on) the Idea—is ethically and creatively "negated" in favor of a "democracy-of-thought" that gives neither the idea nor the object of aesthetics priority. Likewise, the matrixial operation takes both the photograph and the spontaneous philosophies of the image as a superposed model for art-thought. Again, this superposing of the two is an ethical and aesthetic effort. "The artist of philo-fiction" aims to clone the "insurrectional and creative plane of art, creative precisely because its most dominant finalities are taken out of play."[29]

Art's openness to interpretation—its suspension of interpretive finalities—constitutes an insurrectionary force that photo-fiction (and its related practices) ethically mime. "Photo-fiction is not a technological and perceptual act of photographing," Laruelle explains, "but a theoretical act 'miming' the material act but which is irreducible to it."[30] Photo-fiction must be as open to interpretation as art without forfeiting the rigor and exacting conditions of philosophical practice. "Generic and quantic writing," writes Laruelle, "implies that ecstatic depth itself is overridden like the relief on a photo. As if the spontaneous and doxic relief of thinking was annihilated and resurrected by an insurrectional subtraction of words."[31] Passages like these make for difficult reading. Their obscurity "implies" an "ecstatic depth"—like the depth of a photo—at once illusory and strangely real. The words lose their traction (subtraction) in the surface depths of photo-fiction. They retain their immanent autonomy—as the *photo qua photo* does—and at the same time they point to a place outside its rhetorical matrix. The moment words fail the test of intelligibility, or lose their traction in the Real, they enact an insurrectionary violence against the tradition of Platonic aesthetics and ethics. The relation between ideas and art in the field of non-philosophy is rendered as a radical duality without dualism. It reframes or matrixes the relation as a radical parallelism. Laruelle writes:

> Philo-fiction is a gushing and subtractive usage of the means of thinking, of philosophemes-without philosophy, of mathemes-without-mathematics, and from here, all of the dimensions of philosophy are rid of their proper all-encompassing finality, an insurrection against the all-too great superior finalities.[32]

Laruelle's practice of non-aesthetics reconstitutes the subjectivist vantage of aesthetic theory from a "scientific" perspective. The depersonalizing pressure exerted on artistic raw material circumvents the humanist trap that ensnares the theory of art in a theory of human subjectivity and essentialist expressivity. Laruelle's "scientific" vantage secures the possibility and potency of "art-thought" instead of thought about art. But this thought that is art is no longer to be seen as the materialized thought of the artist or the critic as standard aesthetics has it. Laruelle's method, again, is to discover the "hypothesis" in art and to play out that hypothesis in a speculative venture of writing that is at once a practice in aesthetics and ethics. By working with the raw materials of science and art, Laruelle draws an ethical measure. For aesthetics "conditioned by the discoveries and methodologies of science," writes Tilford, "should cease to be understood as a subjective and privileged mode of access to the Real in favor of its intelligibility as a multimodal artifice of cognition."[33] Tilford precisely grasps the implications of Laruelle's sense of science. The hypothetical proposition immanent in the material and discursive situatedness of the artwork is the thought that non-aesthetics is ethically compelled to think. It is not a truth, but a *question* immanent to the work external to the life of the artist and resistant to philosophical domination. To take seriously that art is a "hypothesis" is to credit the immanent intellectuality of the artwork even when this intellectuality, as often, is presented in sensual form. The artwork for Laruelle is a *res cogitans*—a thinking thing—a form of "cognitive technology" or "cognitive engineering."[34] The ethical imperative of philo-fictive practice is to wrest the "science" of art from the ideology of humanist sentiment.

The labor of art

We have seen how non-aesthetics superposes ethics, aesthetics, and philosophy even as it is irreducible to any of these. But there is also a political dimension. This aspect of Laruelle's work is comprised of the raw materials of Marxism, but a Marxism voided of its standard philosophical trappings. This section explicates the politics of non-aesthetics through a non-Marxist examination of the "work" of the work of art—the labor of art.

Laruelle's most explicit statement on politics is his *Introduction to Non-Marxism*. There Laruelle identifies standard philosophy with capital. At first, this may seem a stretch. But the logic is clear. Standard philosophy operates by appropriating to itself materials and practices. It is this acquisitive and possessive aspect of standard philosophy that Laruelle identifies with the ethos of capital. Non-Marxism's aim is to emancipate raw materials and practices from standard philosophy's acquisitive domination. But he also seeks to emancipate Marx from Marxism. Laruelle's starting point is effectively Marx's own statement that he was never a Marxist. The appropriation of Marx's emancipatory philosophy by Marxist philosophy is non-Marxism's chief meta-critical task.

The point of intersection between non-aesthetics and non-Marxism is the labor of art. Standard aesthetics appropriates art and extracts a "surplus value" in the form of an increase in the cultural capital of standard philosophy. The labor of art—its sensuous and intellectual work—is exploited when it is made a subject of philosophy. But, Laruelle's non-Marxism is not simply an indictment of the acquisitive attitude of standard philosophy. Non-Marxism, as a clone of non-philosophy, reproduces and reaffirms non-philosophy's first axiom. The Real as One is ontologically non-relational in contrast to the "exchange-based economies" of standard philosophy, which continually profit on exchanges between being and thought, world and word, true and false, meaning and nonsense, and so forth. Standard philosophy rests on a "principle of sufficient economy" that insures its decisional effectivity.[35] This capitalist principle, notes Galloway, "renders all fixity as permeable and reversible."[36] But for Laruelle something is irreversible: the Real. The Real is causally determinant in a unilateral and unidirectional manner. The Real cannot be exchanged for any philosophy for it is the very condition of possibility for philosophy or thought of any kind. The Real enters into no relation and thus no exchange with any thought. Non-philosophy is ontologically non-capitalist in this respect.

Non-Marxism retains a materialist orientation but voids materialism of its philosophical determinations. To philosophically determine what is truly material and what is truly immaterial would only reproduce a *philosophy of materialism*. Materialism for Laruelle includes everything like linen, coats, bricks, but *also* all those "raw materials" of philosophy. The "real basis" of Marx's work is the Real. Laruelle writes:

> The drive to make Marx intelligible, of making him acceptable according to the philosophical norms of acceptability, has led to completing him instead of un-encumbering him, of taking away from him his postulates which are useless. . . . If the "philosophical" problems of Marxism have a philosophical origin or cause, it will suffice to resolve them by determining the ensemble of its apparatus through the radical immanence of the Real.[37]

The resolution of Marxism's philosophical problems can only be resolved by "determining" the Marxist "apparatus" in light of the "radical immanence of the Real." The hunt for "philosophical" solutions engender "useless" postulates that simply pile up on top of those of Marx himself. The truly radical solution is to insert Marx's work into the framework of the radical immanence of the Real. From this vantage, the viewpoint of "vision-in-One," the "real" world of Marxist struggle and the struggle to emancipate Marxism appear as co-equal tasks. World and word of Marxism are Laruelle's raw material; "raw" because it is philosophically unrefined. The "materiality" of non-Marxist materialism is of the Real, which is to say a "real-without-philosophy."[38]

The appropriation of raw materials by standard philosophy or what Laruelle calls "thought-capital," constitutes the "economic" base of standard aesthetics. The objects, practices, and spontaneous philosophies created by the labor of art are systematically appropriated by "thought-capital" and its cultural capital is capitalized through the reproduction of the system of exchange that we call *the philosophy of art*.[39] The conceptual conditions of this system of exchange normalize and naturalize philosophy's principle of sufficiency. Philosophies of art presuppose that they have sufficient resources to determine the value of art or aesthetic achievement. The "crises" and controversies that arise in the standard philosophical economy serve only to auto-valorize it. It matters less which philosophy is dominant and which not than that the philosophical system of exchange continues. The key task of a non-Marxist aesthetics is to break with the ideology of exchange reified in standard philosophy. This task will not be accomplished by instituting another philosophy. As Laruelle cryptically notes:

Non-Marxism is not . . . the substitution of a new philosophy as a better foundation for an old one. Marxism already possesses its philosophy, it has all too much of it. And it is the global position and the usage of this philosophy that it is a matter of evaluating, as encompassing, the materialist break and later, on the basis of this material, as a simple *support* inside this new theory.[40]

What is needed is a "new theory" that will take as its object both the philosophy of Marxism and its "global position." What is required is a "materialist break" with the materialism of standard Marxism and a new materialism derived from an immanent "vision-in-One" of the Real from which the relations between thought and world literally do not "matter" for they are seen to be immanent to the radically Real. We need then a break with philosophical materialism, and on the basis of this break, to construct a non-capitalist thought.

This new theory of "raw" or simply non-philosophical materialism would then constitute the basis for a new unified theory of non-philosophical materialism that will creatively negate the dialectic between material thought and the material world. This has radical implications for art theory.

The standard "exchange relation" of art and thought and its domination by "thought-capital" is to be abolished. Laruelle ultimately accuses standard philosophy as a form of thinking that in its very movement reproduces and reifies capitalist principles of exchange. Philosophy "is constituted in a fashion perfectly analogous to the one which grounds capitalism," writes Katerina Kolozova, in her study of non-Marxism, "philosophy constitutes a reality in its own right and a reality that establishes an amphibology with the real."[41] To better understand Laruelle's non-Marxist project and how it shapes his non-aesthetic practice requires that we dig a little deeper into the raw materials of Laruelle's non-Marxism. The primary source for non-Marxism lies in the raw materials furnished by Althusser. And thus, we must return to Althusser's famed "return to Marx."

The identity of "theory": Laruelle after Althusser

Althusser's "return to Marx" in the mid-1960s was a theoretical return. Marxist theory was in shambles. Stalinism had dealt a deadly ethical blow to it. Khrushchev's call to recover Marx's "true humanism" took refuge in the works of the young Marx. The French Communist Party (PCF) followed suit. Marxist-humanism in short order became the reigning ideology of the PCF. Althusser (and his students) rebelled by setting about on a left-wing critique of Stalinism and Marxist-humanism. Althusser saw both as deviations from Marx's "science." The young Marx was pre-scientific. It was the later Marx of *Capital* that had to be philosophically understood if Marxist theory was to be renewed.[42] Althusser's first move was to show that the science of Marx was entirely incompatible with humanism. It is not the "human" subject that lies at the center of Marx's work, Althusser argued, but the concept of "class." Classes make history.

The first objective of Althusser's theoretical struggle was thus to rid Marxist science of humanist ideology. Althusser was ethically committed to do justice to Marx's emancipatory science. The ethical tone of his project rings in lines like this. "We thus have a categorical duty to treat Marx's theory (in its two domains: historical materialism and dialectical materialism) as what it is—a true science."[43] Marx's science of history (historical materialism) was "true" but its philosophical foundation (dialectical materialism) was incomplete. "Whereas Marx was able to develop [the science of] historical materialism," writes Althusser, "he was not able to do the same for *dialectical materialism, or Marxist philosophy.*"[44]

Dialectical materialism had to be completed to reestablish Marxism's scientific and political legitimacy. A sound Marxist philosophy was needed to prevent the further collapse of Marx's science into ideology. And that meant it had to be *treated as a science* open to "development and research."[45] Althusser sought to resist the "hidden danger" inherent in treating "Marxist science as a *given* or a set of finished truths" in an "empiricist or *dogmatic* fashion."[46] Stalin's reign had frozen research and development of Marx's science. True destalinization, Althusser argued, would require more than a change in the leadership of the Soviet Union and a thawing of its repressive state apparatus. Marxist science would have to be scrubbed clean of its ideological contaminants. "Theory" was to accomplish this by drawing from and beyond the Marxist tradition. To be faithful to all that makes Marx's science "theoretically revolutionary," writes Althusser, requires a "struggle against the ideologies that continually threaten to suffocate, reduce, and destroy Marxist thought."[47] To present Marx's thought as a fixed tablet of final truths was to philosophically aid and abet the weaponization of Marxist thought at the hands of repressive state apparatuses in the Soviet Union and elsewhere. Theory was the order of the day. But for theory to be successful would require that it have the freedom necessary for research and development. And this freedom necessitated the freedom to theorize the role of theory itself. What was needed in the first instance was a working theory of Marxist theory.

A theory of Marxist theory required specifying its identity and its relationship to Marx's science. Althusser struggled with this problem throughout his career. But one theme is constant. Theory is to be understood as a practice that *produces* knowledge and not as a *reflection* of final truths. In, *The Spontaneous Philosophy of the Scientists*, Althusser notes:

> To know is not to extract from the impurities and diversity of the real the pure essence contained in the real, as gold is extracted from the dross of sand and dirt in which it is contained. To know is to *produce* the adequate concept of the object by putting to work means of theoretical production (theory and method), applied to a given raw material. This *production* of knowledge in a given science is a *specific practice*, which should be called *theoretical practice—a specific practice, distinct, that is, from other existing practices* (economic, political, ideological practices) *and absolutely irreplaceable at its level and in its function.*[48]

Theory is understood not as the method by which to "extract" preexistent truths. It is a "specific practice" that "produces" knowledge by putting theory "to work" on "raw material."

Althusser's concision conceals a problem. To know is to theoretically *produce* adequate concepts. And Althusser specifies that theoretical production is a "specific practice," but his theory of "theoretical practice" is trapped in a vicious circle. If to know is to practice theory, then to know what theory is requires practicing a "specific" practice, namely, "theoretical practice." But to know the nature of "theoretical practice" requires producing "adequate concepts" precisely through the labor of "theoretical practice." This wheel-in-the-mud reasoning is symptomatic of Althusser's ethical desire to close the theory/practice split. This desire is a defining feature of the Marxist tradition as a whole. Marx's aim to not merely think but change the world instituted a deep and abiding concern to bridge theory and practice in a unified "praxis" at once philosophical and political in essence.

Althusser's effort to produce a "theory of theoretical practice" was as much an effort to theorize *theory* as it was to theorize *praxis*. He wanted to situate theory as a material practice of production as a counter to idealist ideology. Yet this effort was troubled from the start. His theory's reliance on the theory-practice dialectic demanded a dialectical intervention that cannot lead to theoretical completion for the nature of dialectical thought is incomplete. Althusser's attempt to close the theory/practice split "auto-positioned" his theory within the framework of dialectical materialism from which it could not escape.[49] "Theory" in Althusser's discourse appears to be a "symptomatic" term. It insistently surfaces and disappears back into the logic of his texts. It marks a stressed conceptuality for it names at once a commitment to thought and a desire to transcend it.[50]

In a recent and remarkable essay, Alain Badiou tracks the "vanishing" trace of "theory" in Althusser's *Reading Capital* in which the stated specificity of theoretical practice is diffused throughout by a set of words that mark its iterative and uncertain definition. "A sort of *retour du refoulé* (return of the repressed)," writes Badiou in a Freudian tone, "the disparition of the unity of the word 'theory' is paid for by the appearance of many words that lie within the vocabulary of the philosophy of science. And the most important of these is that of 'knowledge.'"[51] Badiou precisely articulates the stakes of Althusser's privileging of "knowledge" in the context of "theoretical practice." Badiou writes:

> The characteristic activity of theoretical practice is the production of knowledge. . . . After the disparition of theory, we have the appearance of knowledge, and with the appearance of knowledge, we have the appearance of thinking, and thinking is the name for the element or the space of the process of the production of knowledge. . . . Where do we encounter this process of production, the production of knowledge? The answer is: this production of knowledge occurs in thinking. Thinking is . . . the common characteristic of all theoretical practices, the common element, the common place.[52]

Badiou turns the tables on Althusser's method of reading by carrying out a "symptomatic reading" of Althusser's use of the word "theory." "Theory" signifies a haunting "return of the repressed," of "thinking," which is to say that what returns and recurs iteratively through the repetition of "theory," is the specter of Hegel, the specter of idealism, if not of "idealist ideology." Badiou drives home his analysis by citing Althusser himself. In *Reading Capital*, Althusser writes: "The production of knowledge . . . constitutes a process that takes place entirely within thought."[53] Of this passage, Badiou notes, that it is a "very dangerous expression" because "to be *entirely in thought* is to be outside the Real."[54] Althusser's attempt to destroy the dialectical relationship between theory and practice symptomatically resurfaces insistently in the theory-practice (and philosophy-science) dialectic, which itself gives rise to a haunting Hegelianism that dangerously threatens to destroy Althusser's materialist foundation. Badiou notes that Althusser's "materialist guarantee" for "theory" resides solely in the "metaphoric use of words like 'production,' 'mechanism,' 'apparatus,' and so on."[55] Althusser's attempt to anchor his floating signifier, "theory," to firm materialist grounds symptomatically compels his textual production to specify the materiality of "theory" through select metaphors, which is to say that this anchoring is achieved through an *aesthetic practice* invested in the use of figural language to secure a materialist basis for theoretical practice.

How then does Laruelle respond to the problem of the *theory of theory*? He affirms Althusser's desire to emancipate Marxist theory from dogmatic Marxism. The decisive difference, however, between their work concerns the relation between theory and its "raw material." The "raw material" of concern to Althusser comprises the data of the science of history as materialized in class struggle. Theory is the means of production necessary to "produce" concepts "adequate" to the data of history. The "raw material" of concern to Laruelle is that of philosophy itself. Theory is the process of extracting from *philosophy's raw material* concepts deprived of their decisionist bearing on the Real or "clones" with which to repopulate and transform philosophy in non-standard ways. Althusser's "theory" produces a philosophical image of the World auto-positioned by the Marxist theory-practice dialectic. Laruelle's theory decouples the thought-World dialectic and thereby displaces the theory-practice dialectic. Althusser is a theorist of the philosophical World. Laruelle is a theorist of the World of philosophy.

Laruelle's perspective has radical implications for resisting the acquisitive and possessive power of philosophy over art. But in order to see how, we have to take a closer look at how Laruelle challenges the domination of "thought-capital" over other forms of thinking not recognized as sufficiently "philosophical."

Laruelle's axiom that philosophy is insufficient to grasp the Real *necessarily* grants theoretical practice a degree of relative autonomy.

"Rescuing Marxism from metaphysics," writes Laruelle, "is effectively an illusion as long as it is not rescued from philosophical sufficiency itself, belief in the Real and desire for the Real."[56] But, and this is key, *the gap between thought and the Real is immanent to the Real itself.* Laruelle radicalizes the duality of Althusserianism or "dualyzes" the theory/Real split in a radically immanentist hypothesis. The split between the Real, and the insufficiency of thought to grasp it, is located in the Real itself. All thought (philosophical, scientific, aesthetic, political, and so forth) is equally insufficient. Seen from the radically immanent perspective of "vision-in-One," philosophy appears as raw material that is equally insufficient as all other modes of thought and practice. It is not that Marxism (or any other philosophical tradition) is to be rejected. It is to be defetishized, but not demolished. Laruelle writes:

> How do we make philosophy a simple *contribution* equal to the others, with its sufficiency removed from it, if not by determining it in-the-last-instance by the Real which is as non-political as it is non-scientific and non-philosophical? The *non-* cannot have any other "content" except that of the radical immanence of the Real or strictly following from it, without being a relation of negation to philosophy itself and co-determined by it (or by class struggle, etc.). We will invert—at least—the usual approach of a philosophical appropriation of Marxism. Rather than completing Marxism through axioms drawn from the tradition . . . we will instead disappropriate every constituent relation to philosophy (but not its materials, symptoms, and models), i.e., every relation to it that is itself philosophical.[57]

Laruelle clones the democratic aspirations of Marxism in order to institute a democracy of (and in) thought that can at the very least parallel the possibility for radical democracy. Democratic thought begins for Laruelle with the axiom that all thought is equally insufficient to grasp the Real. This is not relativism. It is a principled position that respects the equal insufficiency of thought to grasp the Real. Taking this democratic principle as a point of departure, Laruelle calls for a radical divestment from "thought-as-capital" or, we might say, the *cultural capital of philosophy*, maintained and reproduced by its institutionalized ideology, as thought sufficient and adequate to the Real. Philosophical "materials," "symptoms," and "models" are retained, but with their "sufficiency removed." Such a democratic vision of thought parallels in "thought-world" the radical, democratic, and emancipatory potential and potency of Marxist politics. "At bottom," Laruelle asserts, "it is a matter of dismantling the Principle of Sufficient Marxism not through history, capital, and philosophy altogether but, on the contrary through a non-sufficient conception of the real base and infrastructure."[58] Here Laruelle clones and mutates two of Marxism's most revered and contested terms.

What is called "vulgar Marxism" conceives modes and relations of production as the Real: the "base" of the "superstructure" of thought in all its forms. This has long been challenged by Marxists from Gramsci and Lukács to Althusser and Jameson and many others. But Laruelle mutates this by challenging the sufficiency of the "real base" of Marxist philosophy itself and the ideological infrastructure that binds its theses and drives its internal crises. Laruelle is committed to dismantling the cultural capital of Marxism as a *philosophical project* in order to reconstitute its emancipatory potential for thought and for political practice. Laruelle's perspective of radical immanence rewrites the "base-superstructure" formulation as "base-infrastructure." The vulgar Marxist presupposes the Real to be equal to the real modes and relations of production and thought as its superstructural outgrowth. The standard model is a two-story architectonic. Laruelle, by contrast, axiomatically takes the Real as One as the "base" and thought as its immanent infrastructure. Laruelle's model is a flat plane. Laruelle's ethical project is to answer Marx's call for philosophers to change the world by radicalizing Marx's method.

> We do not oppose a doctrinal regression to these philosophically saturated forms [of Marxism], but rather a non-Marxist practice of Marxism . . . struggle[s] against the "particular interests" of philosophical systems desperately attempting to capture it, and this can already be seen in Marx's work. The error would be in believing that the suspension of . . . philosophical postulates, the suspension of [sufficient] philosophy itself . . . amounts to a regression into economism, into a thoughtless and vulgar Marxism.[59]

The practice of non-Marxism is a struggle against the postulate of self-sufficient Marxism, which is itself only a specific instance of the auto-positing by philosophy of its sufficiency to grasp the Real. To read Marx as a non-Marxist is to resist at once the denial of the Real and the temptation to decide it. It is to be attentive to the shared and lived experience of being "human" as an effect of the Real. It is to be on guard against the victimization of other forms of thought including art. It is to resist the reproduction of philosophies of exchange that extract cognitive "surplus value" through which philosophy's cultural capital is further capitalized. From the radical perspective of "vision-in-One," thought and object no longer appear in a dialectical sequence or in an order of priority. They are radically equal inasmuch as they are equally part of the "infrastructure" of the Real.

Laruelle's "unified-theoretical" perspective "does not reactivate a hidden possibility" dormant within the raw material, but instead performs a reading "adequate to its [non-philosophy's] style" by "making itself out of a heteronomous discovery."[60] Every instance of non-philosophy must rediscover this "non" that is an "effect" of the Real. "Different from a philosophy," non-philosophical "theories demand that they not be relatively 'forgotten,' superseded, reactivated by and for another," writes Laruelle, "but transformed in a heteronomous way by this 'non-' that is the effect of radical immanence."[61] Non-philosophical practices are "limited interpretations or models of a more universal theory" and this is precisely also what becomes of "the philosophies they are woven from."[62] The cultural capital of non-philosophy and standard philosophy is "reduced" by the axiom of radical immanence. Each is merely a part of the infrastructural totality of the Real.

All this is laudable. But can non-philosophical theory answer Althusser's question in its own terms? What is theory? What specifies the theoretical specificity of non-philosophical practice? Katerina Kolozova brilliantly rises to the occasion in her reading of Laruelle's non-Marxist theory. In *Towards a Radical Metaphysics of Socialism*, Kolozova attempts to do for Laruelle what Althusser attempted to do for Marx: to render a *theory of theoretical practice*. She writes:

In non-standard philosophy, the term "theory" refers to thought's transcendental substratum, which can be rid of philosophy or of the authority of philosophy. . . . There is a perfect parallel between

Marx's use of "theory," for which he also often uses synonyms like "philosophy," "abstraction," and "speculation," and Laruelle's use of the term "philosophy." Marx argues for a materialism that will not be philosophical in the last instance, but rather one that will cause the meaning of the term to vanish.[63]

The "transcendental substratum" of thought is the Real. The Real is the immanent plane that conditions thought but transcends its finitude. Marx used theory as a "synonym" for "philosophy" and "abstraction." Marx sought to "rid" thought of "philosophy" so as to think materiality in materialist terms. Laruelle uses "philosophy" in a "parallel" way to how Marx used "theory." Philosophy decides on the Real and projects a World made in its own image. This World is an abstraction. Non-philosophical practice radicalizes Marx's admonition against "philosophy" by reinserting it into the immanent logic of the Real. Put simply: there is no theory of non-philosophical practice any more than there is a philosophy of Marx.[64] To reprise Badiou's incisive critique of Althusser: the "vanishing" of "theory" in Althusser is symptomatic of a stalled attempt to vanish the problematic of the theory of theoretical practice by an overcoming of the theory-practice dialectic. From the perspective of "vision-in-One," this very problem vanishes in the vanishing of dialectics itself. This "vanishing" of the problem is in part an *aesthetic* solution. The vanishing of theory is operationalized less by theses and arguments than by an axiomatic style.

Non-philosophy seeks (and sustains itself though seeking) a *style* adequate to the axiomatic assertion of the Real as that which is foreclosed to full epistemic access and a correspondingly axiomatic assertion of the radical insufficiency of every philosophy. While it makes ample use of available raw materials, non-philosophy is not, Laruelle insists, an "assemblage," a "medley of colors," or a "postmodern crossbreeding," despite its appearance at times to the contrary.[65] Any raw material "can function as a 'source' if it is no longer considered as it is given empirically in its original environment" for it is only through the cloning procedure that is also a mutational transformation that non-philosophy can be articulated.[66] And what is articulated in the "fictions" of non-philosophy is a prose style immanent to itself that parallels and is decided in-the-last-instance by the Real. The transformative effect of cloning philosophical and other raw materials enables the immanent power of fiction to force open perspectives otherwise foreclosed by the representationalist paradigm of thought "on" the Real. "By dissociating fiction from any claim to *approximate* reality," writes John O' Maoilearca, fiction's "own radical Real can emerge."[67] But what is it that binds and gives form to the "identity" of non-philosophical fiction?

It is firstly by the adoption of tactics (syntactical, grammatical, rhetorical, imagistic) that non-philosophy and its fictional forms consistently elide the trap of deciding "upon" or speaking "of" the Real. These stylistic strategies preserve the axiomatic frame of the Real as foreclosed to (yet decisive for) any and all thought in the last instance. These strategies can result in texts by Laruelle, or photographs by Cameron, or readymades by Duchamp, or the plays of Michael Frayn. What all these share is that they do not claim to decide the Real of philosophy or photography or art or atomic physics. They do not decide the nature of their objects. Rather, they transform the practice of textual and visual production by foreclosing the question of the nature of their respective objects. Michael Frayn's *Copenhagen*, for example, takes the materials of science, the politics of nuclear energy, the historical trauma of Nazism—all very real—and clones them into a dramatic fiction out of which a new set of insights emerge that can in no way be reduced to the materials he used, but neither could this immanent identity have emerged without them. *Copenhagen* changes nothing of what actually happened in Copenhagen in 1941; makes no statement concerning the science of quantum physics; and makes no revision to the historical record. Instead, it realizes its own *immanent truth as fiction* determined by all that was actual and potential on a certain day in Copenhagen in 1941. It stakes its theoretical wager on Frayn's "Thucydidean principle" that fiction *alongside* (and not to the exclusion) of the Real is necessary to reveal what empiricist ideologies obscure: epistemic insufficiency with respect to the historical Real—where "recorded and recordable history cannot reach"—"is indeed the substance of the play."[68]

Cameron, Duchamp, Frayn, and Laruelle are non-philosophical practitioners inasmuch (and only inasmuch) as they immanently resist the fables of sufficiency to represent the Real while simultaneously enabling this very insufficiency to radically orient their focus. Together this constellation of thought and image may be said to form a "unified theory" but unified by a *democracy of thought* by virtue of the shared epistemic insufficiencies of each. Such a "unified theory," writes Laruelle, "is not a strict or narrow form of synthesis" for synthesis is of the order of amphibological, which is to say, "philosophical" thought, but instead constitutes a "parallelism of attributes (aspects) that we will call radical rather than absolute—a parallelism . . . [to] the (side of the) One [that is the Real]."[69] The task of non-aesthetic theory is to seek out this kernel, which is to say, in a certain sense, the work's autonomy and freedom from philosophy and ideology and its *unilateral non-relationality* to the Real. "Laruelle's project aims to be unilateral in approach," writes Anthony Paul Smith, "not to think from difference but to think from identity or radical immanence."[70]

Photo-fractality

Non-philosophies partake in a generic "democracy of thought" that respects the autonomy and equality of thought on the grounds that different forms of thought differently manifest epistemic insufficiencies. The identity of non-philosophy is thus marked by a structural invariant, but this invariance can take many forms. The image that best captures this is the fractal.

Laruelle's references fractals and "fractality" throughout his work for it fittingly captures non-philosophy's identity: many forms immanently linked by the structural invariant of epistemic insufficiency. Laruelle's fractal form is frequently matrixed with photography in his writings on art and aesthetics. Photographs can look very different from one another, but they are all immanently structured by the invariant conditions of photography itself. Fractality is also an instance of Laruelle's "science fiction" insofar as the "raw material" of algebraic geometry is cloned in order to produce a form that *looks like* mathematics but is devoid of its decisional structures. Invoking the name of Benoit Mandelbrot, the mathematician who invented the term "fractal," and who devoted his professional life to understanding it, Laruelle argues that the photographic image constitutes a relation of infinite irregularity between the look of the photo and the act of looking at it. "A photo 'looks,' must be 'looked at,' and the wholly internal drama at play harbors a new concept of fractality. . . . We shall call it a 'non-Mandelbrotian' or 'generalized fractality.'"[71] This "generalized fractality" also applies to non-philosophy itself. Non-philosophy is a fractality of fictional forms unified by the structural invariants of non-philosophy's axioms.

Fractality is a science fiction that superposes the aesthetic and scientific matrices of algebraic geometry (science) and photography (a scientific art), but there is also an ethical dimension to fractal forms of non-aesthetics. For if aesthetics "is the claimed domination of philosophy over art," as Laruelle claims, then non-aesthetics is the emancipation of art from philosophy and from its "class position" beneath the historically sovereign supremacy of philosophy from Plato to Hegel and beyond.[72] The "insurrectionary" force of non-philosophical fiction is its aesthetical and ethical power to undermine this presupposed and institutionally validated supremacy of philosophy. It is important to note that Laruelle is careful to consistently use the term "insurrection" and not "revolution" for the purpose of non-aesthetics is not to *overthrow* the tradition of philosophical aesthetics. Indeed, non-aesthetics is reliant on the raw materials provided by the former. Rather, the point is to productively disempower and deprioritize philosophy's domination over art. Laruelle writes:

> We propose another solution that, without excluding aesthetics, no longer grants it this domination of philosophical categories over works of art, but limits it in order to focus on its transformation. It's about substituting for the conflict of art and philosophy the conjugation of their means regulated on the basis of a scientific model. We will . . . explore the following matrix: non-aesthetics or non-standard aesthetics as the reciprocal determination of art and philosophy but [through] . . . the algebraic coefficient present in (quantum) physics.[73]

This abstract and somewhat opaque formulation of the aesthetics and ethics of non-aesthetics is an instance of the non-aesthetic matrix in action. Quantum physics and mathematics are presented here in a form of science fiction superposed or in a relation of "reciprocal determination" with art. Neither philosophical aesthetics nor the science of physics is revolutionized, but rather both are reduced to raw materials and fictively matrixed in an irreverent and insurrectionary mode.

The frustration that Laruelle's work can elicit should perhaps be seen as a parallel to the difficulties that attend the interpretation of "difficult" works of art. We have seen already in the previous chapter how Adorno, Benjamin, and Derrida set important precedents for Laruelle's work. Each strived to elaborate an inventive response to the intellectual challenge of "difficult" art. They have in their own ways delineated a practice of aesthetics (or non-aesthetics) which *parallels* (or clones) rather than replicates in words works of art. They challenge the traditional division of labor between artists and critics— where the former *makes* and the latter *interprets*—for an avowed parallelism in which critical and creative practice is superposed. Laruelle writes:

> In photo-fiction [or non-aesthetics generally], all the language used . . . becomes impossible or unintelligible not due to the excess or surreptitious over-determination by the world, but because of an under-determinant or subtractive usage by a higher language of philosophy that has become ordinary language, having lost its most esoteric and sublime sense.[74]

The aesthetics of non-aesthetics employs language in a "subtractive" way to undermine standard philosophical rhetoric and the repressive pressure it exerts on creative-critical thought. Standard aesthetics "claimed domination" over art by the power of judgment works by rhetorically refusing creative play thereby distancing its voice to achieve a pseudo-objectivity. Laruelle's call for a creative practice of aesthetics underscores the emancipatory labor of art. Art provides for a "displacement of the angle of vision" in Walter Benjamin's words.[75] It has the potential to displace the angle from which we see history, reality, politics, and more. It enables us to see that another world is possible.

Laruelle places more than a degree of utopian hope in art and artists. The labor of art is a labor of visualizing the possible in material form. Art signifies the possibility of invention. It gives form to alternate ways of thinking and being. And it is art's spirit of invention and inventiveness that non-aesthetics clones into its syntax and style. Non-aesthetics affirms art's capacity to escape decision as the immanent sign of human freedom under conditions of unfreedom and inhumanity. Thus, Laruelle's non-aesthetics intersects with his ethical theory. His ethical theory is rooted in what he has called the "human-in-person." This is the human of concrete and lived life. It is not the human given under philosophies of humanism, anti-humanism, or posthumanism. It is the concrete human that transcends the limiting conceptual framework of all philosophies of the human. The human is beyond what can be finally and fully decided by any conceptual apparatus. The human like the Real is beyond philosophy and in this narrow respect is formally a "metaphysical" concept.

Metaphysics

Laruelle's commitment to the concrete human is strongly averse to the general consensus of postwar Continental philosophy. His generation of thinkers sought in various ways to decenter and deconstruct "the human" by pointing out its historical ontology and its normative constellation: white, male, Anglo-European, Western, and capitalist. From Althusser's "theoretical anti-humanism" to Foucault's disappearance of "man," to Derrida's "animality," to Lyotard's "inhuman," to Haraway's "cyborg," to the "posthumanist" politics and ethics of Rosi Braidotti and others, we have witnessed a near wholesale abandonment of "the human" as concept and category in postwar theory. Laruelle has been one of the few holdouts. But, Laruelle resists the tendency to aggrandize or dethrone "the human" via an essentialist gesture that *decides in advance* what it is to be human. Laruelle takes aim at (pro and con) philosophies of the human. In *Dictionary of Non-Philosophy*, he writes:

> Philosophy wants the inhuman, the pre-human, the all-too-human and the over-human without recognizing the "ordinary" nothing-but-human. The philosophical heavens are teeming with anthropoid creatures . . . spawned from a cloven thought and leading a host of masks and travesties which, after that of the demons and angels, is hardly more rationalized. Humanism [and posthumanism] is an

inferior angelism and a lie about man. Philosophy is not so easily saved from this dishonor by the thesis of theoretical anti-humanism (Althusser) that will not have been sufficiently radicalized.[76]

The "philosophical heavens" are teeming with philosophical abstractions of the human.

But what philosophy cannot think, Laruelle insists, is the actual, lived life of human existence. Why are there so many philosophies of humanism of both affirmative and critical varieties if not because none of them are sufficient to conceptually grasp the radically real of human existence? "Man," writes Laruelle in an especially marked passage, "is precisely the Real foreclosed to philosophy."[77] The "human" and the "Real" occupy structurally parallel positions within non-philosophy: both are foreclosed to full epistemic access, which is to say foreclosed to all forms of Philosophical Decision.

The affirmation of the human is not a matter of Philosophical Decision for Laruelle: it is an axiomatic commitment. Non-philosophy defines the human "in a 'formal' way but without formalism."[78] This purely axiomatic formalism ethically affirms the human without prior appeal to philosophical criteria. Laruelle refuses to submit either the human or the Real to the limiting constraints of Philosophical Decision. To be human is an immanent condition rooted in the Real. The human and the Real are thus logically rendered formally "transcendental" in non-philosophy. To be human is to be "in" the Real and thus by Laruelle's lights to be *beyond* the reach of Philosophical Decision. As Gangle and Greve put it:

> The aim or objective of Laruelle's work may be described in general as the honing of a *human theoretical stance* that would no longer objectify the human in the manner of philosophy or its disciplinary avatars but would instead proceed within and among the materials given by such disciplines via a method of immanent theory, or generic science.[79]

Non-philosophically, to be "human" means to accept that there is no final theory or philosophy of the human any more than there is a final theory or philosophy of the Real. Yet this also means the possibility of working with philosophies of the human as a material to render a new alien sense of ourselves, or what Laruelle calls the "stranger-subject." "Non-philosophy has finally found in the Stranger," writes Laruelle, "its strategically most adequate concept of man [or the human], more precisely of the subject as existing beyond the real immanence that it moreover is in its ultimate cause."[80] The *experience* of being human is "beyond" the immanence of the Real *only* in the sense that no experience can grasp the radical immanence of the Real even as the Real is its "ultimate cause." The Real and the human set the cardinal points of non-philosophy's ethical compass. But these cardinal points are non-analyzable in the last instance. Kolozova thus rightly identifies an ethic of "non-analysis" at the heart of Laruelle's project. "The real of the human-in-human, according to Laruelle's non-analysis," writes Kolozova, "inevitably mediates itself through the process of estranging oneself from the real that one is."[81] The human and the Real are given without that "given" of phenomenological postulation, for to be a "real" human being is to be a stranger to oneself.

Laruelle's ethics of the human affirms the making of art and the making of thought into a form of art or "fiction." His work superposes the abstraction of "pure" formal theory, the sensuous "subtraction" of words from routinized meanings, but it is at the same time an affirmation of all that is concretely real. Non-philosophy is purely formal. But its formalism is voided of philosophical formalism. The relative autonomy of non-philosophical thought immanently emerges in the gap between the Real and its effects and between the human-in-human and the human "subject" of philosophy. Kolozova rightly identifies non-philosophy as a "metaphysical" project in the last instance. It is so in two senses. First, it axiomatically asserts that the Real and the human are "beyond" all thought. This gap immanent to Real secures a measure of freedom from the Real inasmuch as no thought is adequate to the Real. Thus, in a strange sense, the Real and thought are "beyond" the reach of either. It is in this sense that non-philosophy can be understood as a recommencement of metaphysics in the age of its deconstruction.

Laruelle's project starts with a minimal metaphysical postulation: the Real is foreclosed to full epistemic access. Laruelle rigorously elides pronouncing anything about the Real beyond its epistemic foreclosure. But still this axiomatic starting point is a metaphysical one.

Kolozova brilliantly locates this irreducible metaphysical dimension of Laruelle's project in his reading of Marx. Kolozova writes:

> If "giving up our [philosophical] abstractions" is the central and most important tasks of the science that Marx invents and attempts to institute, then I would argue that the following task should be to emancipate . . . metaphysics . . . from the authority of philosophy. It is the primitive and radical metaphysics of the inevitable gesture of mediating the immediate real that ought to be salvaged through non-philosophical scientific operations with the *chôra* of metaphysical thought.[82]

The "*chôra* of metaphysical thought"—all that thought the West had so confidently exiled from the philosophical kingdom of twentieth-century philosophy—is reaffirmed in Laruelle's insistence on the gap between thought and the Real (even while this gap is immanent to the Real). The Real is beyond decisionist thought and in this minimal way it retains a relative autonomy from the Real and is thus "metaphysical" by definition.

To reprise, non-Marxism, non-aesthetics, photo-fiction, art-fiction, science fiction, philo-fiction are not all the same thing, but they share an underlying axiom: standard philosophy alienates the human-in-human by converting it into a "subject" of philosophy whose grandeur rests on its claim to know the Real. From this vantage of supreme abstraction, philosophy has justified immeasurably inhumane measures. In the name of "Marxist truths," it has justified genocide; in the name of scientific truths it has justified the atom bomb; in the name of aesthetic truths it has consolidated canons of exclusion; in the name of humanism it has justified inhumanity; in the name of objectivity it has justified objectification. Everywhere philosophy has stipulated justifications it has justified its own existence in the last instance at the expense of what it claims to represent, speak for or in the name of. It cannot tolerate a thought that exceeds its warrant.

Non-philosophy is not a destruction of philosophy. Such a teleologically oriented project of destruction would do nothing more than reproduce the very form of philosophical domination through alienation that non-philosophy desires to suspend. It is, again, a matter of treating philosophy and science as raw materials—as a *chôra* of competing and incomplete conceptual finitudes—with which it is possible to compose forms of thinking and writing hitherto excluded from the kingdom of philosophy. It is a matter of preserving philosophy while letting go of its supposed sufficiency and right to rule. No longer is philosophy to be the king as in the Platonic conception. Non-philosophy institutes a "democracy of thought" that looks as much to science, art, and political practice as it does to standard philosophy itself in order to think according to (and not on) the Real.

Review

We have explored quite a bit in this chapter. Let us take a moment by way of conclusion to review. We recall that the principal axiom of non-philosophy is radical immanence and the Real as foreclosed to full epistemic access. This grants what Laruelle calls the "fiction" of non-philosophy a "relative autonomy" from the Real while nonetheless being determined by it in the last instance. Non-philosophy rejects the Principle of Sufficient Philosophy upon which the signature gesture of philosophy is inscribed: Philosophical Decision. No decision can be taken on the Real for the Real is what is decisive for thought in the last instance. We have also explored the aesthetics of non-philosophy— its fictive modes of exposition—and their bearing on the work of traditional aesthetics. Looking to the precedent of writers, including Adorno, Benjamin, and Derrida as well as the work of artists such as Duchamp, Cameron, Frayn, and Rauschenberg, we examined how non-aesthetics opens a parallel perspective on the relation between art and art theory. Contra the decisional impulse of standard aesthetics, non-aesthetics seeks neither to decide the ontology of art nor to judge aesthetic competence. Rather, its aim is to "clone" the aesthetic "raw material" of art into a "matrix" of art and science, but not to mix the two and thereby reproduce hackneyed amphibologies. The matrix does not mix or blend the raw materials of art and science. It instead *reproduces* them in cloned forms that grants the Real of science and of art its autonomy by fictionalizing aesthetic theory. *Non-aesthetics is not a theory of art, but an aesthetic practice of theorizing.* Non-aesthetics offers neither commentaries nor critiques: it clones and parallels. In the next chapter, we will more closely examine this cloned parallelism.

4

Aesthetics in a Different Light:

Kapoor, Flavin, Turrell

This chapter examines the problem of non-philosophical decisionism and "force (of) thought" through three case studies in the art of light and reflection: the art of Anish Kapoor, Dan Flavin, and James Turrell. It begins with a consideration of the problem of decision in non-philosophy: the "force (of) thought" by which it *decides against decision and standard philosophy* in one stroke. I argue that this "force (of) thought" is operative in the above case studies and this force, in turn, forces the critical act to respond as a mime or a "clone" of this very force. The chapter concludes by turning to the question of art's relation to the critical act by reframing that relation as a non-relation in light of the force (and foreclosure) of the Real.

Non-philosophical decisionism

The problem of decisionism in Laruelle's work is not lost on Laruelle himself. He knows full well that to decide against the imperatives and ethics of Philosophical Decision is to decide in a radical way against philosophy. Laruelle acknowledges this problem. In *Introduction to Non-Marxism*, he writes that non-philosophy "contains an essential part of decisions."[1] Laruelle suggests that there is no escape from a certain decisional impulse. For Laruelle, what must be resisted is the fall into Philosophical Decision on the Real. Put simply: non-philosophy *decides against deciding on the Real and against philosophy for doing so.* Non-philosophy relies on an ethic of pure decisionism inasmuch as it decides against deciding on the Real. Its decisionism is axiomatic and global. But nothing other than axiomatic insistence grounds Laruelle's reduction of philosophy to Philosophical Decision on the Real. The compelling force of non-philosophy is given in the form of an axiomatic "force (of) thought." Laruelle defines "force (of) thought" as "the first possible experience of thought—after vision-in-One."[2] It is a "complex thought" says Laruelle, but in essence that thought is "caused" by the Real for it is immanent to it. This is not an "abstract" concept so much as an "experience" of this forcing of thought by the Real. This "force" of the Real is "thought" by cloning its force through forceful (sometimes forced) axiomatic thought. Non-philosophy's axiomatic force is defended by Laruelle as the cloned condition of the force of the immanently Real on thought. This is signaled in the syntax of the clone "force (of) thought" itself. The "of" in "force (of) thought" is placed in parentheses to signal that the force of thought is not "of" thought as all thought is *in* the Real. And it signals that the split between the force *of* the Real and its conceptual correlation is immanent to the Real. Effectively, there is no "of" in the actual relation between the force (of the) Real and thought, for there is no relationality within the radical immanence of the Real that is One. As Anthony Paul Smith explains: "Thought is produced and determined-in-the-last-instance by the One, which is not a thought."[3]

Laruelle's axiomatic decision to identify standard philosophy with Philosophical Decision, and his decision to identify non-philosophy with its suspension, is decisive in every respect. It is of the essence of non-philosophical decisionism that it is a "pure," groundless, or "sovereign" decision precisely because it is axiomatic through and through. Its compelling force lies not in elaborate argument, but in its rhetorical and syntactical "force (of) thought." The clone "force (of) thought" thus names a decisional imperative to force a suspension of belief in philosophical sufficiency. Writing in a Marxist register, Laruelle notes in *Philosophy and Non-Philosophy*:

What is to be done, and how do we proceed more concretely? One can no longer remain content with suspending, as limited or exhausted, the average or statistical axioms that ground a given [philosophical] age—such as ours—if not a philosophical community. . . . It is necessary to suspend the *belief-in-philosophy* that supports . . . fairly massive slogans, the spontaneous belief according to which, for example, there is a logos or logocentrism, and there is the Other or the Undecidable. Rather than practicing them naively, we should question why we uphold these axioms and the absolute authority we confer upon them.[4]

Here Laruelle explicitly targets deconstruction's critique of logocentrism and its ethical demand to orient thought according to the Other. Laruelle asks that we question the universalizing axioms that stabilize the projects and objects of philosophical critique. For critique, as Baudrillard pointed out forcefully, always magnifies the power of that which it critiques.[5] The temptation to fall into standard philosophy is very great especially for one trained in philosophy like Laruelle himself. He knows all too well that "what is to be done" is *to decide against* the pseudo-domination of the Real.

Non-philosophy is an activity, a doing, that in and through its various "fictions" immanently and iteratively enacts a decision against standard philosophical decisionism. We might inflect this with more nuance by countenancing Julius Greve's insightful reading of the "decisional apparatus" in Laruelle's work. Greve's contention is that Laruelle's anti-authoritarian ethics is immanently reflected in a practice that insistently aims at uncovering the decisional apparatus operative within a given philosophical, aesthetic, or scientific regime.[6] But this very aim is decisive and determines the character of the non-philosophical signature. As Anthony Paul Smith notes, "Non-philosophy's own practice emerges from a mutation of this decisional structure in an analogous way to the emergence of non-Euclidean geometry."[7] But, as Smith and Laruelle know, non-Euclidean geometry *is founded* upon an entirely different set of axioms from those formulated by Euclid. The alternative axioms of non-Euclidean geometry, like those of non-philosophy, are a set of decisions that break with the classical postulates of both fields of thought and endeavor. Non-philosophy, like non-Euclidian geometry, changes the shape of what can be thought by deciding to found a new axiomatic starting point. Non-aesthetics is also founded on a new axiomatic that firstly refuses to decide on the nature of art or aesthetic achievement as in standard aesthetics. But, importantly it is also reshaped by the axiomatic "force (of) thought" immanent to art itself.

That the materiality of art is also the materiality of a certain concept of art is the immanent thought that connects the art of Duchamp to the Conceptual Art movement of the 1970s and a host of contemporary art movements today. Joseph Kosuth, one of the preeminent pioneers of Conceptual Art, followed Duchamp's example by calling attention to the irreducible conceptuality of material works of art. In his landmark essay, "Art after Philosophy," Kosuth argued:

> The value of particular artists after Duchamp can be weighed according to how much they questioned the nature of art; which is another way of saying "what they *added* to the conception of art" or what wasn't there before they started. Artists question the nature of art presenting new propositions as to art's nature. And to do this one cannot concern oneself with the handed-down "language" of traditional art, as this activity is based on the assumption that there is only one way of framing art propositions.[8]

Kosuth's post-Duchampian theory of art holds that material artworks have an irreducible propositional content. Each artwork proposes that it is itself a work of art and thus proposes also a possible "definition of art."[9] Every artwork proposes a concept of art through its very existence as a work of art. Kosuth's title is telling. "Art after Philosophy" is an essay concerned with the historical fate of art "after Duchamp." Kosuth credits Duchamp's *art as philosophy* inasmuch as it materially proposed that the reconceptualization of art's nature could itself become a form of art. Kosuth argues that the "value" of artists "after Duchamp" should be measured by how "much they question[n] the nature of art" or "what they ad[d]" to the concept of art. But Kosuth did not articulate a new theory of criticism on the basis of this.

Kosuth's conceptualist theory displaced the art-thought dialectic. But it did not displace the art-philosophy dialectic. Kosuth took as self-evident that the philosophical question raised by art was that of art's definition. This left philosophy in charge of deciphering what concept of art a given artwork advances. Moreover, Kosuth failed to consider to what extent art could change not only the definition of art but also the concept of philosophical art criticism itself. If, as Kosuth argues, every artwork proposes a concept of art, then it falls to philosophy to determine or decide what that concept is. The radicality of Kosuth's position is seriously undermined by its unwitting avowal of the prioritization of philosophy over art. The art of Anish Kapoor, Dan Flavin, and James Turrell (to which we will turn shortly) challenges this prioritization in surprising ways. There are to be sure many other artists who do as well. But the work of these artists exerts a "force (of) thought" on "philosophical" concepts: "reflection" (Kapoor), "history" (Flavin), and truth and illusion (Turrell).

Reflection (Kapoor)

The art of Anish Kapoor forces reflection on place and displacement. His work has consistently explored the relation between place and displacement by working with mirrors, fragile materials, echoes, and voids. Reflection, piling, accretion and removal, citation and caesura establish an aesthetic and ethic of translation, transition, of the contingent movement through the space and time of the contemporary global epoch, and the annals of transnational history. Kapoor's post-minimalist economy of expression condenses the complexities of global translation and transition into a vocabulary of suggestive forms and brilliant colors set in and out of the gallery. Indeed, many of his most celebrated works are works of public art.

Undoubtedly, one of the best commentators on Kapoor's work (other than Kapoor himself) is Homi Bhabha. In "Elusive Objects," Bhabha situates Kapoor's work as an "elusive" and transfigured sign of cultural displacement. Bhabha and Kapoor both came of age in the postcolonial condition of India of the 1960s and 1970s. The Bombay cultural scene at that time informed their complexly cosmopolitan and postcolonial ethics and aesthetics. The chaotic cosmopolitanism of Bombay at that time was marked by the remainders and reminders of British colonialism sitting side by side an emergent, independent cultural scene. Bhabha writes:

The Bombay art scene, as I remember those energetic, emergent years, made no claims to aesthetic or civic order; everybody was caught up in the pell-mell project of trying to survive. What held it all together, despite marked social differences, was the sense of a post-colonial avant-garde—tilted away from orthodoxies, eastern and western—co-existing in an excited atmosphere of innovation and experimentation. We lived with this jagged reality of cultural juxtapositions—the sclerotic, scholarly Museum and the seething gallery culture. And we learnt to manoeuvre within the social disjunctions that mapped the city's everyday life: wealth and poverty, beauty and squalor, the intellectual and the illiterate, caste subservience and class struggle.[10]

Bhabha contextualizes Kapoor's art in the light of the postcolonial art scene of Bombay of the 1960s and 1970s. But Bhabha is quick to remind his readers that any attempt to situate Kapoor's work *solely* in the psycho-geographies of postcolonial India risks defaulting into a "sentimental exercise in establishing the artist's 'authenticity' . . . rather than a critical engagement with the 'authority' of the work."[11] It is worth quoting Bhabha again at length on this point.

A work's authority depends less on its aesthetic genealogy than on its ability to catalyze a fissionary process across a field of objects. If authenticity focuses on protecting the sovereignty of form and tradition, authority is established performatively, through an efficacious splitting of the art-object into iterative "nodes" of influence that establish new networks of signification, and new formal possibilities of construction. Authenticity favors the *transmission* of tradition; authority enhances the *translation* of tradition. Indeed, the artist himself has recently written, "There is no hierarchy of form, but form has a propensity to meaning. *And meaning is the translation of art.*"[12]

Bhabha critically displaces the authority of authenticity for the authority of the work of art. Bhabha situates the work immanently within its own corpus as a "fissionary process" that works "across" the "field" of Kapoor's art-objects. The "authority" of Kapoor's work lies in the translational process or *fission* by which the post-minimalist tradition is displaced and translated (rather than simply transmitted) as a set of "iterative nodes" that opens the work beyond the authority of formalist hierarchies. The authority of the work of art—its immanent sovereignty—lies precisely in its forced translation of the tradition from which it appears to descend whether as a genealogy of form (Minimalism) or the psycho-geography of the artist's cultural and historical location (postcolonial India). The sovereign decision to translate genealogy into a new "meaning" constitutes the authority of the work of art. Not blind reproduction and transmission of the authenticity of tradition, but translation establishes the autonomous authority of the work as a site of decisive power.

Bhabha's critical reading effectively clones and parallels the sovereign decisiveness of Kapoor's work by critically displacing the authenticity of tradition in order to constitute a critical voice that parallels the sovereign authority of Kapoor's work by an "efficacious splitting" of the object of critique from the art of critique itself. Bhabha's critical "manuouvre" formulates an "elusive" parallelism with the "authority" of Kapoor's art. Bhabha signals the authority of the work by allowing it to enable a critical reflection on their shared postcolonial memory of the Bombay cultural scene of the 1960s and 1970s. Kapoor's art of postcolonial reflection is itself reflected in Bhabha's criticism. This parallelism honors the conceptuality of Kapoor's work and compels a point of view that is surely "philosophical," but not of the sort envisioned by Kosuth's ontologically oriented theory. Bhabha's critical act "mirrors" the "fissionary" process of Kapoor's serial art of migration, place, and displacement through a reflection on the emergence of Bhabha's "independent" critical voice. Bhabha's essay does not decide what "concept" of art is at issue in Kapoor's art, but what concepts it makes available to thought. He immanently reflects these concepts back by putting them to work on issues that extend far beyond the narrow confines of the ontology of art. Bhabha does not reflect on Kapoor's art in the standard sense. Rather, he engages in a reflection on culture using the concepts immanently inscribed within the serial and fissionary forms of Kapoor's works. Bhabha's essay articulates a non-aesthetic theory of Kapoor's art inasmuch as it is axiomatically determined by the presupposition that Kapoor's art is already a philosophical reflection on place and displacement. The essay responds to that philosophical content by reflecting the work's power of reflection itself by a reflection on the cultural conditions that shaped the artist and the critic's early lives.

Let us further explore this parallelism of reflection by turning to Kapoor's *Sky Mirror*, a work on (and of) reflection *par excellence*. The work is, in fact, part of a series and thus exist in a multiplicity of intertextual relations with other iterations of the work or what Bhabha identifies as the work's status as a "series-being." The London version is set in a park where the moody sky above is displaced by the angle of reflection and the firmament is reframed in that oldest of optical technologies. The formal doubling of pond and mirror ramifies *reflection* as a material and metaphor of thinking nature in the age of mass culture and public life. It is a distant and displaced echo of a process that began in the nineteenth century when the park as a substitute for nature entered the cultural imaginary of artists and spectators alike who wanted to "get away from it all" without ever crossing the city limits. The Impressionists' taste for parks and gardens, for example, served as a living metaphor for the bounded terrain of the canvas where nature is ordered and shaped. The inescapably entwined condition of culture and nature—or "nature-culture" in Donna Haraway's memorable phrase—found expression in images of the burgeoning ranks of the urban middle class enjoying the outdoors *within* the city.[13]

The ascendancy of the landscape in Impressionist art stemmed from two centuries of *reflections* on land as subject and symbol. The work of the seventeenth-century artist, Claude Lorraine, set an important precedent. Landscape in his work is made the carrier of the historical mythology of the fall of naked and "savage" innocence into a "civilized" body-politic. Lorraine made use of mirrors in the making of his work. Using a small, oval glass or a "Claude Glass," Lorraine would work not from the scene in front of him, but from the scene behind him as it appeared reflected in the glass. The looking glass framed, focused, and bounded the image, making the reflected scene into a vignette of nature. *Sky Mirror* descends from this genealogy of landscape art in which the mirror as technique and technology played a central role. But the *authenticity* of the work as a late work of landscape art is displaced by the *authority* of the translational and transformational force of Kapoor's intervention. *Sky Mirror* translates the landscape of post-imperial England into a "post-medium" form of the contemporary global condition. The London that surrounds the park is a living allegory of a cosmopolitan global London and no longer the Eurocentric metropole of the nineteenth century.

Kapoor's work enacts what Benjamin might describe as a "displacement of the angle of vision" by reframing the sky of nature as a cultural cutout mirrored and metaphorically doubled in the form of a generic aesthetic and ethic of displacement: the standard signature of the contemporary and cosmopolitan condition. Benjamin's profound and profoundly elliptical comments on the "displacement of the angle of vision" are found in "On the Theory of Knowledge, Theory of Progress," or "Convolute N" of his *Arcades* project. The poignant and suggestive phrase emerges in the course of what Benjamin calls a "modest methodological proposal for the cultural-historical dialectic."[14] The dialectical tension between the desire to seize on the newness of culture without either sundering it from history or falling into historicism sets the scene. Benjamin notes that the cultural historian will look for the "positive" element in culture as distinct from the "negative" and retrograde background of the banal and status-quo. But such a partitioning of the positively new from the culturally retrograde is insufficiently dialectical for Benjamin. What is "decisive" is to see and seize upon what is new in that very background. Thus, a new method is called for. Benjamin writes:

It is therefore of decisive importance that a new partition be applied to this initially excluded, negative component so that, by a displacement of the angle of vision . . . a positive element emerges anew in it too—something different from that previously signified.[15]

Benjamin provides a useful way of thinking the superposed aesthetico-critical form forced to the fore by Kapoor's *Sky Mirror*. The work materially displaces the image of the sky, but it also critically displaces the concept of "reflection" from the cognitive to the aesthetic and material plane. The work itself enacts a critical act of reflection voided of a human subject. The work materially "reflects" on reflection immanently. The work displaces the epistemological primacy of human reflection to the object. Kapoor's sculpture is an aesthetic and critical object that "displaces the angle" of relation between art and standard philosophical aesthetics. It materially enacts a thought concerning reflection on the public space in post-imperial England. It creates then both a crisis and an opportunity for critical reflection on the work. The work's "force (of) thought" forces standard philosophical criticism back on its heels. The productive problem it critically poses is how to reflect its critical reflection without neutralizing its critical power by subordinating it to standard philosophical decisionism.

Christopher Langlois argues that such self-reflective and self-critical artworks induce a crisis concerning the role of criticism itself. Langlois names this critical condition "terror" and in so doing has restored terror's *conceptual* rights in a courageous refusal to allow neoconservative ideology to constrain and constrict the conceptual challenge of terror by reducing it to non-state-sponsored "terrorism."[16] The conspicuously self-critical artwork "hijack[s] the labor of interpreting," writes Langlois, and presents itself as a "self-hermeneutic enterprise."[17] Kapoor's *Sky Mirror* forces open the problematic by critically doubling the act and art of reflection. It instates the possibility and potencies of displacing standard philosophical aesthetics for an art of simulation, mirroring, doubling, miming, or *cloning* the artwork in question. What is critically terrifying about such an apparently placid work like *Sky Mirror* is that it reduces the critical act of reflection to a clone. But, it is precisely in this forcing of the critical voice into a strange doubling of the work that *Sky Mirror* displaces the authority of philosophical reflection by an aesthetic of reflection. Kapoor's work displaces the angle of relation between art and philosophical aesthetics and instates an insurrectionary "force (of) thought" upon the standard relation between the two. As Laruelle notes in *Photo-Fiction*:

> Aesthetics, particularly since Hegel, is the claimed domination of philosophy over art by which philosophy claims to unpack its meaning, truth, and destination. . . . In its least aggressive, least legislative form, philosophy describes art's figures, eras, its styles, the formal systems according to philosophy's own norms. Art for its part always rebels. We propose another solution that, without excluding aesthetics, no longer grants it this domination . . . over

works of art, but limits it in order to focus on its transformation
[read—cloning or mutating]. It's about substituting for the conflict
of art and philosophy the conjugation of their means.[18]

Two temptations are to be resisted: reification of non-philosophy
or of art. The point is to give neither priority, but to superpose their
decisional powers and take the critical measure of this matrixed or
conjugated art-thought object by applying it to domains *beyond* art
and aesthetics as Bhabha does in his "elusive" essay on Kapoor. In
the terms in which we are working here, the solution lies neither
with Laruelle nor Kapoor. The solution lies in superposing the two and
taking *that* as the critical object. Not Laruelle nor Kapoor, but Kapoor/
Laruelle as an instance of "fictionally" unified fractality would be the
point of departure.

   This fractal structure of superposition also reformats the question of
prioritization. No longer is it a question of art before philosophy or the
inverse. The structural superposing of the two in conformity with the
radical thesis of the immanence of the Real as One enables a "force
(of) thought" to emerge that envisions the "relation" between art and
thought in rigorously non-dialectical terms. From the perspective of
"vision-in-One," there is no longer an economy of exchange between
art and thought and therefore no specter of domination at the hands
of "thought-capital." What is seen from the perspective of "vision-
in-One" is no longer art on the one side and thought on the other.
Rather, what "appears" is "art-thought" as the inadequate name
for the immanent unification of the two in the last instance by the
Real. In the context in which we are working—Kapoor and Laruelle—
we could say that the artwork, *Sky Mirror*, and its non-philosophical
double (the question of reflection) are not interchangeable. They
exist as a "superposition"; neither gives rise to the other and thus
the question of priority is deprioritized. But this deprioritization is
possible only because art and thought, seen from the perspective of
"vision-in-One," are unified by virtue of the immanent causality of
the Real in the last instance. The practice of non-aesthetics affirms
the "authority" and the autonomy of art and thought as superposed
conditions of the Real without collapsing one into the other in an
authoritarian confinement of one by the other. Yet as noted there is
still a moment of decision—a moment of decisive *recognizability* in

Benjamin's poignant phrase—that inheres even in non-philosophy. To decline to decide on the Real and to decide against philosophy—for doing this is to decide, nonetheless. But it is to decide on something *different* than standard philosophy decides upon. We will return to this matter of the non-relationality of art and theory soon. But for the moment, let us move on to examine another light artist—Dan Flavin.

History (Flavin)

Flavin was committed to working with Light and Space using only commercially available fluorescent light fixtures. His spaces are suffused with fluorescent oranges, pinks, greens, whites, yellows, and blues set in minimalist, geometric arrangements. His constructions invert the traditional museological schema between artwork and exhibition space. The gallery does not illuminate the artwork; the artwork illuminates the gallery as a phenomenological and ideological construct. Flavin exposes the fact that gallery space is not simply physical, but psychical, historical, and ideological; it is also a space that demarcates an institutional judgment concerning the artwork's significance and cultural validity. And this logic extends to the viewer who inhabits the space too. "Perhaps the most important site that Flavin's work engages," writes J. Fiona Ragheb, "is that of the viewer's subjectivity."[19] Flavin's "acknowledgment of the contextual frame in which the art work was perceived," Ragheb continues, "interpolated the viewer into that context."[20] And that "context" is, again, at once physical, psychical, historical, and ideological, or we might say in a Laruellean register, that the space is in a state of "superposition." This extended context is one in which the entire body of the viewer is interpolated through the light as it casts its "seductive glow on the spectator's skin."[21] Flavin's work (like other Minimalists of his generation) delocalizes the art-object by literally dispersing it in the form of a suffusing glow that fills the entire space. The art of Flavin's constructions exists in the relation between the viewer's body and the architectural site. The light serves as the aesthetic point of connection and interaction between the two. But once the lights go out, and the viewers leave, the "art" disappears. The art is at once site-specific and time-specific. Flavin's art is not simply there. It *happens* only in and through a specific set of spatial and temporal relations with the surrounding space and the viewers.

The form of Flavin's radically non-representationalist work is set into dialectical contrast with his titles, which "while usually untitled, are typically accompanied by dedications to his family, friends, colleagues and . . . to historical figures like Brancusi, Henri Matisse, Mondrian, [and] Vladimir Tatlin."[22] Ragheb argues that Flavin's dedications "insist on a sentiment and warmth absent from the prevailing rhetoric of Minimalism."[23] This is no doubt true, but what is contestable is Ragheb's further claim that it is "here among the proper names of Flavin's dedications that place reemerges, forming an autobiographical constellation of touchstones that describe the artist's personal and professional life in abbreviated form."[24] Ragheb all-too-easily collapses the constitutive tension in Flavin's work between the personal and the abstract, the sensuous and the intellectual, skin and site, place and space into an "autobiographical constellation" of the "artist's personal and professional life." The place of the transpersonal and the historical in Flavin's work is effaced in Ragheb's standard art-historical reading of Flavin.

Flavin's engagement with art-historical names is a way of thinking about history. His politically critical and philosophically inclined mediations on history and meta-history come to the fore in his homages to the famed Russian Constructivist and ardent Communist revolutionary artist, Vladimir Tatlin (1885–1953). Flavin made a series of homages to the artist between 1966 and 1970. They all consist of seven white fluorescent tubes of varying lengths arranged in different vertical assemblages. Let us examine Flavin's *"Monument" 1 for V. Tatlin* of 1966 (Figure 5).

The steeple-like shape rises to a central spire of light, bathing the surrounding space in a haze of pure, white light. The title sets the work's Minimalist identity adjacent to the historical space marked by the revolutionary art of Tatlin, who coined the term "Constructivism" to name his project and that of his fellow Russian avant-garde artists loyal to the ideals of the October Revolution. The term "Constructivism" was invented to replace terms like "sculpture," "architecture," "painting," or "art" itself, which now appeared ideologically tainted by the epoch of bourgeois cultural domination that the revolution was supposed to have revolutionized. The Constructivists, like Tatlin,

FIGURE 5 *Dan Flavin,* "Monument" 1 *for V. Tatlin, 1964.*
Source: Flavin, Dan. (1933–96). © ARS, NY. "Monument" for V. Tatlin 1. 1964.
Fluorescent lights and metal fixtures, 243.8 × 58.7 × 10.8 cm. Gift of UBS. The
Museum of Modern Art. Digital Image © The Museum of Modern Art/Licensed
by SCALA/Art Resource, NY. © 2018 Stephen Flavin/Artists Rights Society (ARS),
New York.

saw themselves as "constructors" or builders of a revolutionary
visual culture where the lines between "high" and "mass" culture
were to be dissolved into simple, non-representationalist, geometric
compositions whose intelligibility would not depend on the viewer
having any knowledge of the visual rhetoric or narratives of "high"
art. All that would be necessary to "understand" Constructivist work,
Tatlin hoped, was a familiarity with the geometric and chromatic
vocabulary of young children.

The most important of Tatlin's constructions is his *Monument to
the Third International* of 1920. The structure was to be Moscow's
answer to the Eiffel Tower. Rising in corkscrew fashion at a 45
degree angle, the monument was to be a functional structure that

would house the high offices of the Soviet bureaucracy in a series of circular floors that would ascend in order of political importance and power. The floors were to rotate on specific dates of importance on the revolutionary calendar. And the roof was to be outfitted with what Tatlin described as a machine capable of writing revolutionary slogans on the sky.[25] The building was never built. But the model became a monument to the movement in its own right. It was carried in parades and celebrations as a revolutionary icon. The monument spontaneously reflected the constitutive tensions of Leninism: the classless society was to be instituted by a highly disciplined party hierarchy; the eventual "withering of the state" would be quickened by an iron-fisted "dictatorship of the proletariat"; true revolution would mean the historical end of class struggle.

The utopian aspirations of Constructivism belied its elitist roots in the transnational currents of aesthetic modernity. What was truly utopian was Tatlin's and the Constructivists's attempt to transvalue aesthetic modernity into a universal, visual grammar of emancipation. That a non-representationalist art of shape and color could be the vanguard art of the working and peasant classes reflected the youthful idealism of the Russian revolutionary intelligentsia. The ebullient atmosphere of the Russian revolutionary avant-garde was, however, soon plunged into the deep freeze of Stalinism. Stalin's promotion of an art of "the people" in the form of grossly, kitschy renditions of chiseled bodies engaged in hard work for the state failed to produce either a credible "socialist realism" or a valid riposte to the Western avant-gardes.[26] The tragedy of Stalinism has recast the light in which we from our historical present view the fleeting utopianism of the Constructivist program. We cannot help seeing it from the perspective of a future that once was. We see in Tatlin's construction a utopia denied.

It is this freighted history that is superposed in Flavin's minimalist and readymade project. He inherits the syntax of Constructivism in the age of depoliticized art; for Minimalism, it must be said, was to become the preferred décor of corporate lobbies at the end of the twentieth century. Only the name "Tatlin" remains in Flavin's art turned into a monument in the ideologically neutralized annals of high formalist art. The Third International for its part is buried without monument. The afterlife glow of Tatlin's art set within Flavin's mass-technology of light *cum* art rewrites the utopian *revolutionary slogans on the sky* in a displaced monument illuminating the dark. There is a self-critical moment superposed within the syntax of the structure and the memorial that Flavin erects within the space of politically neutralized American Minimalist aesthetics. It calls out in ironic voice its neutered state as a monument to art history of the present and not to a Constructivist politics of art in service to a history now long past.

Light has been of central importance to the history of Western art from the Renaissance to Impressionism and beyond. And there is a parallel story of light in the history of Western philosophy. Laruelle is deeply critical of the entire fascination with light in the Western philosophical and cultural imaginary as many others of his generation have been. Indeed, as Martin Jay has so astutely argued, many of the stalwarts of postwar theory, including Lacan, Adorno and Horkheimer, Merleau-Ponty, Althusser, and Derrida, were both propelled and repelled by the philosophic metaphoricity of "light" as illumination, reflection, adequation, reason, and truth.[27] The turn away from vision and light as the governing metaphors of truth went hand-in-hand with the rise of ideological critique and its deeply rooted suspicion of appearance. This suspicion was fed by a deep reservoir of anti-ocular sentiment from Plato through Marx, which held that appearances masked a deeper truth. The same suspicion of appearance underwrote Freud's psychoanalytic project. His so-called "topographical" diagram of the psyche envisioned the conscious mind as the visible tip of a vast iceberg and the "unconscious" as lying hidden from view below the watery depths. In this respect, Laruelle is in lockstep with the general consensus of many philosophers of his generation. But it is arguable that no one has been more ruthless in seeking out the deep structure of "ocularcentrism" within the apparently ocularphobic discourse of postwar theory. The hermeneutics of suspicion that treats appearance as fundamentally untrustworthy belies a belief that philosophy can pierce the veil of appearance to see things as they really are. The critique of appearance under the sign of a critique of the visible is thus generative of another form of ocularcentrism thinly masked by a superficial disavowal of the metaphoricity of light and vision.

Laruelle's strident critique of the link between light and philosophy—so central to the style and consequences of Philosophical

Decision—is found throughout his work but takes an especially acute form in his work on photography. Laruelle strategically clones his non-philosophical critique of ocularcentrism in a discussion of what he identifies as the "onto-photo-logical" conditions of standard philosophy. Through the lens of photography, Laruelle envisions a non-philosophical double that would occupy the same structural relation as a photo does to the Real. Laruelle conceptualizes the photo's appearance as containing its own immanent identity as a photo. This identity of the photo as photo and not as transcription of the Real is Laruelle's axiomatic starting point. And this conception offers him a readymade model for non-philosophy itself. Like non-photography, non-philosophy is an immanent mode of thought that maintains in-the-last-instance a relative autonomy with respect to the Real. Standard philosophy, argues Laruelle, proceeds on the basis of the Philosophical Decision which stakes its grandeur on a self-perpetuating myth that philosophy is sufficient to illuminate the Real. Put shortly, Philosophical Decision operates like a mythological camera armed with the capacity to light-up and capture the Real. The action of this mythical philo-camera reduces phenomena to "onto-photo-logical" essences: reduced to an image of the Real. But this image, Laruelle insists, is a phantasm of the process of Philosophical Decision. The image of the World that it creates is an invention of the selfsame apparatus that captured it—standard philosophy. To break with this *photo-graphy*—this false discovery of the light of reason—begins by first taking into account that the action of the philo-photographic apparatus *produces* its images of the visibly Real. It does not simply "take" them. Philosophy, or theory as Althusser already argued, is *productive*. Theory is a production—an assemblage of techniques—that produces an image of the Real. Just as the sky reflected in Kapoor's *Sky Mirror* is not, of course, the sky itself, so too theory is a reflection *produced* by a theoretical apparatus and is in no way an innocent or objective transcription of the Real.

Laruelle's *theory of theory* is in a sense then the double of *Sky Mirror's* epistemology: it is a reflection of the Real which, precisely because it is a *reflection*, is not in fact the Real itself.[28] Laruelle's point is that a certain "photo-graphy" (a light-writing) traverses the philosophical canon inasmuch as the pursuit of *truth* has been analogically and unconsciously linked to the capture and writing of the light of reason and truth. The philosophical procedure according to which the World is thought to be transcribed as a trustworthy "reflection" in philosophy's "mirror of nature" is transvalued in photographic terms by Laruelle. Philosophy auto-produces an image of the World through the operation of this philo-photo apparatus. But this image is precisely a *philosophical image of the World* that philosophy's optics make possible and not the World and the Real as such. Accordingly, for Laruelle, every philosophy since Plato that has taken the image as untrustworthy is itself to be taken with suspicion for its constitutive blindness to its own image-making or onto-photo-graphical orientation.

Flavin's light constructions rewrite photography *qua* light-writing as it has been encoded within the West's onto-photo-logical orientation in a structured syntax that is *transparently constructed.* "Tatlin" is signified in name only as a depoliticized sign of commercialized and commodified culture and this is further ramified in the mass-produced light fixtures comprising the work. The illumination of the revolutionary slogan is miniaturized and marketed as "Tatlin" in a non-figurative form whose light is commercially fabricated. Dialectically, it recalls the Constructivist project to emancipate art from the fetish character of the humanist art market in which Flavin's work resides. Flavin's non-figurative recasting of Tatlin's monument *as a monument to Tatlin* serves to remind us that the politics of aesthetics to which Tatlin was committed was rigorously anti-humanist and radically non-representationalist. It was, like Minimalism, a "literalist" impulse to make objects that *present* but do not *represent.*[29]

Flavin critically interrogates the historical legacy of Minimalism's formalist geometries by exposing its depoliticized character. By citing the history of Constructivism in name only through the titular invocation of "Tatlin," Flavin draws attention to what survives of emancipatory avant-gardism in the commodified epoch of late twentieth-century American art. "Tatlin" is cloned along with his formalist geometries, but the revolutionary ardor of Constructivism is cancelled by the cool syntax of Minimalism. This is to say that Flavin's work is equally theoretical and aesthetical. It immanently enacts a meta-critical meditation on the depoliticization of Constructivism in the age of corporate capital.

But, here again, we find that the work appears to have beaten criticism to the punch. Flavin's work already *illuminates* a meta-historical problematic. The work seems to auto-reduce the critical act to the status of a clone of what the work already illuminates in its immanent aesthetico-theoretical form. Flavin's "monument" always already articulates a historico-theoretical critique of Minimalism's depoliticized aesthetics by illuminating the chasm between the geometry of revolution and corporate lobby décor. Flavin's monument has already materially realized a critique of the historical displacement of collectivist art by the hegemonic ideology of individualism under late capital. All this is already realized in the inversion of the "monument" to the political signifier of the "Third International" for a "monument" to the proper art-historical name "Tatlin."

How then can non-aesthetics respond to the immanent aesthetico-theoretical dimension of Flavin's work without merely doubling that aesthetico-theoretical content? It can begin from the point of this impasse and think what it would mean to write aesthetics in the aesthetic register of this impasse. In other words, non-aesthetic practice does not need to "respond" to the work itself, but to discover *how to think its own operation in light of the problematic that the work illuminates*. Put shortly, non-aesthetics might name the practice of philosophizing *according to* art. We will return to this question, but for the moment let us turn to one more light artist who Laruelle himself has engaged with—James Turrell.

Turrell (Truth)

James Turrell is an artist who Laruelle has written on with great interest.[30] Turrell hails from the same generation as Flavin and is typically associated with the Minimalist movement. More specifically, he ranks as one of the key figures of the California school of Minimalism called Light and Space. The artists of the Light and Space school, largely based in California, took a softer, more atmospherically inspired, approach to Minimalism. They were inspired (it is said) by the light and seaside landscape of sunny California. The cool colors and atmospheric installations of artists like John McCracken, Robert

Irwin, and James Turrell, in very different ways, sought a more organic and naturally inspired alternative to the rigid and cold geometries of industrial Minimalism typical of those created by New York artists like Dan Flavin.

The artists of the Light and Space school shared the East Coast Minimalists's desire to extend art beyond the bounds of the aesthetic object. The "object" (handmade, fabricated, or readymade) was no longer seen as the sole focus of art. Instead, the entire "situation" including the surrounding space and the viewer's body was understood by these artists as integral to the very identity of art itself.[31] Art was now seen to exist at the interstices of a set of structural relations between object, space, and viewer. Turrell went one step beyond by eliminating the need for a physical object at all.

His move from physical to purely perceptual objects began in the late 1960s. He acquired an old hotel and converted its rooms into ideal spaces for shaping light. He eventually succeeded in producing objects made solely out of projected light. The first series of these light works he called his Cross-Corner Projections. The projections appear to be solid, three-dimensional shapes hanging in mid-air. But they are all expertly lensed light projected on two-dimensional surfaces. It may be tempting to see these projections as a continuation of the Renaissance legacy of illusionism. But the difference is that illusionistic art aims at securing a stable illusion. Turrell's projections are unstable.

Craig Adcock observes that the "Cross-Corner Projections create solid-like forms that seem to occupy a hypothetical region in front of the walls. They seem to hypostatize space itself, despite the fact that in perceptual terms the 'region' of light itself remains labile."[32] Adcock astutely underscores the difference between Turrell's work and the historical legacy of post-Renaissance illusionistic art. When you look at Turrell's projections from certain angles the three-dimensional illusion disappears. The "labile" perceptual dynamic of Turrell's projections also has an important philosophical dimension. Turrell's projections effectively superpose the standard philosophical binary of appearance and truth. There is no *right* way to see Turrell's projections. The work's identity exists equally as a two-dimensionally and a three-dimensionally perceived object.

It is not difficult to see why Turrell's art would appeal to Laruelle's way of thinking. Turrell's supposition of two-dimensional and three-dimensional perception parallels Laruelle's "dualysis" of the appearance/truth distinction. Laruelle's work, like Turrell's, does not "deconstruct" or dispense with binaries like appearance and truth. Both artist and non-philosopher radially "dualyze" the distinction to render a duality devoid of standard philosophical dualism. The duality of thought/Real, what Laruelle calls the "labor of the radical dyad," is "without operation of scission" for in the "last instance" both are immanent to the Real.[33] "Non-philosophy . . . retains a sense of the dual or duality," observes Anthony Paul Smith, "even as it rejects dualism."[34] "This will be, however, a duality that is unilateral," continues Smith, "in distinction to a mixed, equally weighty, or substantial dualism. From the perspective of the One the usual terms found in dualistic philosophies, like thought and Being, are only local effects of a greater dual relation" unilaterally determined by the Real as One.[35]

Turrell's concept of light and that of Laruelle's are also affine insofar as each strives to think light against the truth/appearance duality. The philosophical consequences of this new conception (or perception) of light is that it detaches the materiality and metaphoricity of light from its long-standing association with truth, reason, and revelation. Both artist and thinker resist the "onto-photo-graphical" impulse of Western philosophizing. Turrell's light offers viewers a radical duality of perceptual experiences. But he voids that dualism of the standard appearance/truth dualism. Turrell also "dualyzes" light by casting it in visual and haptic registers. As Craig Adcock notes:

In all his works, Turrell fashions ethereal visual spaces using pure light. From the beginning of his career to the present, he has endeavored to isolate light, to detach it from the general ambient array, so that the basic characteristics of sheer electromagnetic flux can be seen directly, unsullied by the presence of anything else. Turrell creates works that deal at first hand with light's untouchable essence—and the apparent contradiction of "at first hand" and "untouchable" is used here intentionally; he encourages viewers to see in ways that are haptic, as if they could feel light with their eyes, like pressure on the skin of visual perception.[36]

Adcock rightly points out that Turrell's work superposes visual and haptic experience and thereby displaces the philosophical primacy of the visual and its naturalized link to metaphors of light, vision, knowledge, and truth. Here too, it is a question of a duality—optical and haptic experience—*presented as a duality but not as a dualism.* Turrell's *art of negation* negates the philosophical structure of the truth/appearance dualism without collapsing its multiple dualities of optical perspectives and haptic experiences into a singular identity. Its identity is immanently a multiplicity of dualities. Even the chromatic perception of Turrell's "white" projections can vary considerably from viewer to viewer. "Although projected with identical projectors onto identically prepared walls," writes Adcock, "the altered relationships between the spaces and the projections nuance the perceived colors of the various pieces."[37] Here again there is no dualism between the perceived color and the real color: the chromatic reality of the work is its identity as a *dualism without duality* between the "perceived" and the "real."

Laruelle, himself, has written on Turrell's work. In "A Light Odyssey: The Discovery of Light as a Theoretical and Aesthetic Problem," Laruelle focuses largely on twenty-eight etchings by Turrell. The etchings, collectively titled, *First Light*, are something like etched clones of Turrell's Cross-Corner Projections. Each picture shows a bright, white shape hovering in a darkened space. Laruelle was fascinated by the title of the series. Laruelle writes:

Turrell's title "First Light" is ambiguous and can be interpreted in two ways. In the weakest sense it means just what it means, *first light*, the first among many, its own relative position in a continuous order in which it is included. In the strong sense it means *light first*, all the light given at once, without residual or supplement, without division.[38]

Commenting on this passage, Alexander Galloway notes that it is the "second sense, the strong sense," of "first light" that "is most appealing to Laruelle, because it indicates the identity of light as a kind of first givenness, as a raw discovery or invention without supplement."[39] Light as prior to philosophical division or decision is what Laruelle "discovers" in Turrell's work. Laruelle sees in the theoretical and aesthetic matrix of Turrell's work a means of retaining a concept of "perception" without submitting that concept to the appearance/truth dialectic of standard philosophy. "Turrell's light," writes Galloway, "does not orient the viewer. Instead, according to Laruelle, Turrell's light performs experiments on perception and retains perception according to alternative logics."[40] Light is refocused as a unified perception at once aesthetic and theoretical designed to test perception without testing "truth." "Turrell's experimental mandate," Galloway concludes, "is to allow both the artist and the viewer to test perception . . . not to mimic the way in which perception is normalized by philosophy, not to think about perception, but to think *according to* perception."[41]

Our three case studies in light each exemplify art's immanently philosophical and critical value. Each artwork induces a crisis in criticism. How is criticism to respond to work that is already hyper-critical? What more than a mere echo can criticism in such cases be? Laruelle's answer is to clone art's aesthetico-critical dimension. This begins with the reduction of the artwork to conceptual raw material and to reconstruct that material to create thought that departs for an elsewhere beyond the realm of art. The point for Laruelle is not to critique, judge, or comment on such works: the point is to follow it as a model to think in new ways. Kapoor's reflective art, for example, could be cloned in a style that is equally attentive to the constructed artifice of philosophical reflection and thus capable of creatively negating the onto-photo-graphic mythology of standard philosophy. Flavin's meta-historical and politically astute critique of the auto-valorization of art by the practice of standard art history, and the machinations of the art market, can be taken as raw material for a non-aesthetic critique of standard philosophy *qua* "thought-capital" as well as an inducement to challenge the auto-valorization of philosophy by the standard practice of intellectual history. Such a move would take account of the decidedly amphibological condition of the discipline of history of philosophy that (like art history) is always already a philosophical intervention into that history. Finally, Turrell's interrogation of the appearance/truth duality could be cloned in a formal and syntactical style aimed at presenting the Real/thought duality as a dualism voided of philosophical dualism. These are only speculative and suggestive starts, but the point is only to make clear that non-aesthetics begins with a recognition that art offers material resources for thought. This material can be marshaled into new assemblages to produce new objects and materials for non-philosophical thought. Non-aesthetics looks then to art not as an object but as an intellectual material equal to philosophical thought, and by that gesture of recognition, it enacts the ethics of a "democracy-of-thought." The sovereign force of art can thereby become a means for new non-aesthetic decisions in what might be called a *poesis of axiomatics* rather than commentary, critique, or judgment.

Vision-in-One

The primacy placed on "pure" perception in one sense aligns Turrell and Laruelle with the phenomenological tradition. Edmund Husserl, the founder of phenomenology, taught that coming to grips with phenomena, with what appears, requires that we forego deciding whether or not the phenomenon in question is of the order of the Real. What could be called Laruelle's non-phenomenological method "brackets" the Real to work with materials of philosophy and other raw materials. But where non-philosophy takes its distance from phenomenology is in its refusal to dichotomize appearance and the Real. This refusal is located at the deepest metaphysical level of Laruelle's project. Husserl's "bracketing" method still retains a notion of the Real as lying behind appearance. This method affirms the oldest dualism of Western metaphysics—appearance/truth. Laruelle's clones Husserl's bracketing procedure, but he radicalizes it by bracketing out the entire dialectic of appearance/truth in the name of the radical immanence of the Real. Husserlian "bracketing" is cloned by Laruelle as "vision-in-One." This vision is a "fictional" frame that "sees" all dualities of standard philosophy as dualities without dualism in the last instance. "Vision-in-One" is a syntactical and rhetorical placeholder in Laruelle's thought: it reminds us that if we could see from the perspective of the Real then we could see dualities as immanent to the One. But from our immanent perspective "in" the One we can only see dualities as dualisms. This duality without dualism is often rhetorically packaged by Laruelle in the language of quantum physics because quantum phenomena force us to reckon with dualities without dualisms. Superposition is key among these phenomena. Recall that superposition names a state in which a particle can be said to be in more than one state. Let us explore this further with a brief detour through Erwin Schrödinger's famous thought experiment.

Schrödinger was a critic of the concept of "superposition." In 1935, he devised a thought experiment. He imagined taking a cat and placing it in a steel box outfitted with an atomic substance, a Geiger counter, and vial of lethal gas. He then supposed that the atomic substance had equal chances of decaying and not decaying. If it decayed, then the Geiger counter would go off, which in turn would release the lethal gas and kill the cat. If the atomic matter did not decay then the cat would live. The Copenhagen Interpretation of quantum physics says that until the box is opened, and an observation is made, the reality of the system (cat, Geiger counter, and lethal gas) exists in a superposition of states. This means that the cat is both alive and dead. Schrödinger assumed that the absurd results of this thought experiment would put an end to the concept of superposition. But it didn't. It only deepened the strangeness of the relation between quantum theory and "reality."

Laruelle's metaphysics of the Real is like "Schrödinger's cat" in the sense that it encompasses a multiplicity of states in a unified theory. The Real is One but this One is comprised of a superposition of states. One might ask: Is this not just warmed-over Hegelianism? Hegel's concept of the Absolute also preserves and transcends dualities and perceived oppositions. There are certainly moments and passages in Laruelle's thought that seem to support this comparison. But the key difference is that non-philosophy is not teleologically oriented as is Hegel's absolute idealism. There is for Laruelle no way to ever access the Real and know it by philosophical reason. The Real for Laruelle is permanently foreclosed to full epistemic access. Laruelle puts the matter clearly in *Philosophy and Non-Philosophy*. It is worth quoting him here at length.

"Vision-in-One" means first and foremost that henceforth one sets off from the One rather than from the Dyad; that the One is taken as the immanent guiding thread of research; and even that one remains within this immanence from which we can no longer, not even by the World and Philosophy be made to leave.

. . . Vision-in-One then means that we no longer see the World from itself or from a being-in-the-World, but from and in the One's immanence; that we see an object no longer from its objectivity but from and in the One; *and that we see philosophy no longer from itself but from the One ("non-philosophy")*. However, in the One . . . there can no longer be a simple "image" of the object, furthermore supposed "in itself," no image on a surface or a mirror looked over by a third person.[42]

The passage is verbose, but its point is clear enough. "Vision-in-One" is the non-philosophical answer to Husserl's "bracketing" procedure. Husserlian phenomenology begins with the dyad of appearance/truth. It then brackets out the "truth" to focus on appearance. This appearance is then given the philosophical status of a World of appearance or a "life-world" of experience. The whole of phenomenology as a philosophical project is constructed on this dyadic foundation. The "subject" of phenomenology is then able to be cast as what Heidegger called "being-in-the-world," but a World again constituted by philosophical reason.

Non-philosophy begins from the One and not the Dyad. What is "bracketed" out in "vision-in-One" is philosophical reason and the Worlds it gives rise to no matter whether that is the World of phenomenology (Husserl) or the World of existentialism (Heidegger) or any philosophy and its corresponding Worlds. Every "object" is seen from the perspective of "vision-in-One" as immanently "in" the One. Even this "vision-in-One" is both a perspective "from" and "in" the One. To "see" in this way is to describe immanence in immanent terms. Non-philosophy shatters the "onto-photo-logical" image of philosophy as a neutral and objective "mirror" or "surface" that can be observed from a "third-person" perspective. There is no dualism between philosophy as a "mirror" of reality that can be observed from an objective, third-person perspective and the Real. Philosophy and its imaged Worlds are immanent effects of the Real. "Vision-in-One" means seeing all of philosophy—its objects, instances, and Worlds—as immanent to the Real rather than as an objective *account* of the Real. Philosophy and its Worlds are thus seen as materials immanently superposed "in" the Real. But it is important to note that this "vision-in-One" is a vision of the Real seen as the determinant force only in the "last instance." The Real that is "seen" in "vision-in-One" is a metaphorical approximation of the Real for the Real itself is foreclosed to any thought in the last instance. It is this concept of the "last instance" that we should now examine more closely as it is a key concept in Laruelle's metaphysics of the Real and it has important implications for rethinking the standard relation between art and philosophy.

Determination-in-the-last-instance (DLI)

Non-aesthetics is a practice of cloning art's "force (of) thought" into a creative fictionalization of art: *an aesthetic practice of aesthetic theorizing*. It displaces the prioritization of philosophy over art inherent in standard aesthetics. Philosophical aesthetics "responds" to art by seizing it and dominating it by a value system and the act of judgment. Its fundamental operation is acquisitive and domineering. Non-aesthetics works by cloning or miming art through a creative practice of aesthetic theory that parallels the work of art. The operation of non-aesthetics allows the work of art to work on the raw materials of aesthetic theory. But non-aesthetics does not simply invert the standard hierarchy of thought over art for art over philosophy. Non-aesthetics *prioritizes the deprioritization of art and thought*.

Laruelle's ethico-aesthetic task is to democratize the relation between art and thought according to the axiom of the Real given in "vision-in-One." Art and thought are "seen" as superposed effects of the Real that is One. The Real is without hierarchy and devoid of relationality. The Real is non-hierarchized and non-relational for it is that which is immanent to all relations and constructed hierarchies. This immanent "vision-in-One"—an immanent flatland—is the ultimate cause of everything including all creative practice. But this "cause"—this DLI—is not itself subject to any determination (philosophical or otherwise). It is the immanent cause that determines and decides, but only in the last instance. There is no way to trace back to this "cause" for this cause is causation itself immanent to the fabric of the Real. It is not "origin" or "first cause" nor is it "spirit." It can be named but never known in the last instance. Laruelle writes:

Along with the One . . . non-philosophy's central concept
["determination-in-the-last-instance"] . . . distinguishes it from
all other philosophies. It is said of the One's causality as such
or vision-in-One, of the Real in virtue of its primacy over thought
and its objects (like Being). This causality is exerted upon that
which is given [for standard philosophy] and that which serves
as experience for the data for thought-according-to-the-One: a
causality exerted on philosophy itself. . . . It is therefore also the
specific causality of non-philosophy in general. This concept has a
Marxist origin and is here extracted from historical materialism.[43]

DLI is Laruelle's term for the ultimate metaphysical causality of the
Real for all philosophical and non-philosophical thought. All thought
and all the schisms and splits, decisions or distortions it creates are
effectively determinations of the Real. Laruelle notes that DLI has a
"Marxist origin." It is useful to excavate its Marxist origins in order to
better grasp Laruelle's radical theory of causation.

In a letter of 1890, Engels took the Marxist "economists" to task
for reducing his and Marx's work to "economic determinism." He
noted that the economy was determinant "only in the last instance."[44]
"More than this," Engels concluded, "Marx and I never asserted."[45]
Althusser picks up on this one phrase and gives it an unprecedented
theoretical gravitas in his landmark essay "Contradiction and
Overdetermination."

Althusser argues that Marx and Engels's "science of history"
gave rise to a nascent and radical theory of historical causation.
Althusser argues that the economistic idea that historical change
rests on an economic "base," and that this "causes" the formation
of various "superstructures" of religion, politics, ideology, art and
so forth, is itself an ideological construct entirely foreign to Marxist
science. The cause of historical change is always "overdetermined."
Marx had produced a science of history, and with Engels, he had
produced a new theory of causality appropriate to it. Althusser saw
it as his political and philosophical duty to work out this theory's full
implications. Althusser writes:

We must carry this through to its conclusions and say that this
overdetermination does not just refer to apparently unique and

aberrant historical formations . . . but is *universal*: the economic dialectic is never active *in the pure state*; in History, these instances, the superstructures, etc.—are never seen to step respectfully aside when their work is done or, when the Time comes, as his pure phenomena, to scatter before His Majesty the Economy as he strides along the royal road of the Dialectic. From the first moment to the last, the lonely hour of the "last instance" never comes.[46]

The economy never exists in a "pure state" for it is always entangled or superposed with other instances and structural relations. Economics is always in relations with other forces and is thus never itself *the* determinant force. The overdetermined character of relations within a given historical conjuncture is for Althusser a "universal." Overdetermination is the first law of historical change. Althusser radicalizes Marx and Engels's concept of the "last instance" in his claim that the last instance "never comes." Every instance is overdetermined.

Althusser rejects the model of "base-superstructure" for an immanent theory of overdetermined economic, social, and political "structures." But his "structural" theory of Marxism could not satisfactorily explain what gives rise to structural formations themselves. Althusser struggled with this problem for the whole of his professional life. As Ted Benton observes:

Though the provision of concepts with which to think the effectivity of a "structure" on its elements and subordinate structures and all their effects is presented by Althusser as a *problem*, it is hard to see in his attempt to resolve it any more than as a restatement of the question. The outcome of Althusser's prolonged and labored discussion is that the structure of the totality is *nothing other* than its effects, it is, in Spinoza's sense, a cause "immanent in its effects" (just as, in Spinoza's philosophy, God is a cause immanent in His creation: God and nature are identical).[47]

Althusser's theory of structural (or Spinozist) causality founders in attempting to explain the formation of structures through the structures themselves. Structures are at once their own cause and their own effects. It is to this problem that Laruelle responds by radicalizing Althusser's problematic of the "last instance."

In *Introduction to Non-Marxism*, Laruelle writes that DLI "was invented by Marx and Engels for historical materialism, but they did not give us the adequate conception of it, capable of producing all the simultaneously theoretical and critical effects possible for it."[48] "In order to elucidate DLI in our style," Laruelle continues, "would mean making its Marxist forms appear as simple symptoms or models of a more radical concept of causality."[49] The Real, for Laruelle, must be posited as irreducible to any philosophical determination (Marxist or otherwise). Neither economic nor historical structures are wholly determinant: the Real is decisive and determinant in the last instance. The Real encompasses "history," "economics," "materials" and all "philosophies" from "materialism" to "idealism." All these are effects of the Real. The Real—not "history"—is "overdetermined" according to Laruelle. Taking a cue from Althusser's theory of "symptomatic reading," Laruelle effectively argues that philosophy symptomatically reduces the Real to an object that stands outside a subject. Philosophical Decision determines what is determinant of the Real. This "idealist" ideology of standard philosophy wounds the radicality of Marxist philosophy and reifies the power of all other philosophies. Althusser's "error" lies in having looked to philosophy to better Marx. Laruelle's answer is to emancipate Marx from Marxism. Laruelle writes:

> Althusser's "error" . . . is having looked in Marx for the rational [cause] (and so philosophical and idealist) kernel . . . [of the Real] whereas, in every philosopher, it is necessary to identify the real symptomatic kernel [namely, that of the Real]. Materialism, like finalism, technologism, and formalism, is ejected from and by the DLI understood in its universal identity.[50]

Althusser failed to think the immanence of the Real immanently. He, like Marx, was *too philosophical*. The Real cannot be reduced to a "sphere" or an "instance" governed by the World of any philosophy.[51] Althusser's massively important work is not lightly discounted by Laruelle. He recognizes the value of Althusser's attempt to build on and develop Marx's science. What he is critical of is Althusser's "philosophical" effort. "The set of Marxism's theoretical themes and objects, its massively philosophical (because materialist) economy," writes Laruelle, "must be reorganized and otherwise reconfigured to change its theoretical status."[52] Marx's thought must be scrubbed clean of its exchange-based theoretical economy. No longer should it operate on the exchange principle of *philosophical World=Real*. The World imaged in Marx's philosophical camera—his reduction of the Real to the imaged World of productive forces—should be "reorganized" on an immanent basis that will eradicate the dialectics of base-superstructure for that of the radically Real and its "infrastructure."[53]

DLI gives a proper name to the causality of the Real. But this name is itself a symptom of the Real. There is no thought that is not conditioned by the Real, according to Laruelle. A paradoxical identity: DLI is the ultimate cause of which DLI is also an effect. Laruelle acknowledges this albeit in somewhat cryptic tones: "DLI fully deployed is the causality that makes it universally possible for any object X to determine for itself, *but in-the-last-instance*, its own philosophical X (or for example the concept of DLI itself)."[54] Any "object" of the Real determines "for itself," as part of the Real, the very conditions of any thought (or philosophical concept) of the object itself. Thus, DLI is both the "object and cause of its own theory."[55] DLI is an aporetic structure in non-philosophy. But this is in essence unavoidable. DLI is a syntactical and rhetorical approximation—a figure of speech—that marks what is but which cannot be thought in the last instance: the Real as radical immanence that transcends the dialectic of cause and effect. The schism and splits of standard philosophy—appearance/truth, base/superstructure, World/Real, thought/Being, cause/effect, and so on—are "symptoms" of philosophy's attempt to turn the Real into an object of reflection by force of Philosophical Decision. But the Real knows nothing of such splits even that between philosophy and non-philosophy. In the final analysis, in the last instance, even the split between thought according to the One and thought against it, designated by Laruelle as "non(-One)," is immanent to the radical immanence of the Real. Smith captures this precisely. It is worth quoting him at length.

Determination-in-the-last-instance (DLI) is the name given to the causality of the One upon the various instances of non(-One). Traditional [or standard] philosophical explanations of causality always begin with a division between two terms (cause and effect). . . . This separation, in both strong and weak forms, reduces the moment to a relation and that relation will determine the two identities in a reciprocal or dialectical way. DLI refuses the initial division between cause and effect because such a division is unthinkable from the radical immanence of the One. Insofar as there are instances of the non(-One) or things like thought and Being that lend themselves to traditional accounts of causality and dialectical philosophy, from the perspective of the radically immanent One these effects come after the One and do not form a premise of the One.[56]

The Real as One is determinant in the last instance for all thought whether it is in the style of radical immanence or otherwise. The Real is determinant of thought and this determination is unilateral: everything proceeds unilaterally and irreversibly from the *a priori* of the Real. Laruelle's thesis of the Real as determinant of every philosophical or non-philosophical form may appear to lapse back into a determination or decision on the Real. To pose the Real as determinant is to conceptualize the Real nonetheless and to determine its nature as precisely what is determinant in the last instance. Does this undermine Laruelle's program? Yes and no. Yes, because it does make a concept of the Real. No, because the concept of the Real itself is held to be determined by the Real. The thesis of DLI occupies a precarious point in non-philosophy: at once determined by the infra-architecture of non-philosophy and also the determinant condition for the selfsame infra-architecture. DLI as concept is a case of superposition—at once cause and effect.

DLI has profound implications for leveling the standard hierarchical relation between art and aesthetics. Non-aesthetics "reduces" the priority of aesthetics over art by miming or cloning art. Letting art take priority or even become the "cause" of aesthetics is a first step beyond the standard philosophical enclosure of art by philosophy. Yet, as Althusser knew, a mere inversion of terms remains immanently determined by the relation between those terms. The point is to find (or found) a new relation entirely. Here again, Turrell's aesthetic and theoretical discovery can serve as a guiding thread.

Art and philosophy according to "vision-in-One" do not have a dialectical relation. But neither do they have "no relation" for that would simply be the dialectical inverse of the standard dialectical relation. Rather, they occupy a *relation of non-relationality*. This non-relationality also constitutes a non-prioritization of either in temporal or causal terms. Art does not determine aesthetics nor does aesthetics determine art. Neither art nor philosophy has priority in the field of non-aesthetics: each is but a collection of raw materials. To put the matter in Turrell's terms: in the first and last instance, there is only *first light* prior to its split into the "aesthetic" and "theoretical." "In this sense," writes Galloway, "the artist and the viewer [who may also be a philosopher] are *strictly identical*" inasmuch as all parties see/think "*according* to perception."[57]

Laruelle and Turrell recast light as "first light" as a radically unified artistic-theoretical object. This superposed object enacts a "force (of) thought" on the split between art and theory by rendering both as equally insufficient to grasp the totality of light as a sensuous and intellectual experience. Turrell's deprioritization of artist, viewer, and critic/theorist/philosopher realizes a "democracy of thought" and it therefore enacts a sensuous and intellectual critique of the division of labor that organizes and dominates standard philosophy. It is worth pointing out that Western philosophy's suspicion of the arts began with Plato's exiling of the arts from his ideal Republic. Ever since the question of art has been linked with the question of politics. Laruelle's response is to insist on a "democracy of theory" that will liberate theorizing from its totalizing and totalitarian ambitions.[58] Laruelle's reconceptualization of the relation between art and thought as a *relation of non-relationality* offers a model for such a "democracy of theory" for it neither prioritizes art nor theory but submits each term to a democratic thought founded on the axiom of the "radical" immanence of the Real given as One. "For a democracy—lived out or of thought—to be truly democracy, to speak of an equality-in-the-last-instance," writes Smith, "it must not be political, but thought from the position of radical immanence from the Real."[59] Philosophy "politicizes" the relation between art and theory as a relation of priority and in so doing reproduces the anti-democratic impulse ratified by its primarily decisional nature. To realize a "democracy of thought" or a "democracy of theory" within the practices of making, looking, and thinking according to the perception of art requires seeing all parties as equal by virtue of their shared insufficiencies.

Theory of non-aesthetics?

Let us take a moment to reprise and review the main outlines of non-aesthetics. First, non-aesthetics displaces the hierarchical schema of standard aesthetics. Art is not to be defined or explained by aesthetics (or philosophies of art generally). But non-aesthetics does not simply invert the standard schema; it reinvents it through the radical thesis of the Real as One. The Real as One, as prior to the hierarchies, prioritizations, and schisms of standard philosophy, refocuses the problem of the relation between art and thought as the problem of a relation of non-relationality necessarily outside the duality of philosophical prioritization and irreducible to the philosophical distinction between cause and effect. The "relation" between art and thought (as that between cause and effect) is secondary to the primacy of the radical immanence of the Real as One. Non-aesthetics provides the bare outlines for "introducing" democracy into art theory by rescinding philosophy's claim over art. Non-aesthetics works (in part) through the strategy of cloning or miming the conditions of art at the level of its expository style. Through its peculiar syntax, its strangeness as a style, non-aesthetic practice encodes the strangeness of art into its very discourse, scrambling in advance the distinction between art and philosophy upon which standard aesthetics is founded and through which it perpetuates its power and dominance over art.

In radical fidelity to the concept of DLI by the Real, non-aesthetics opens a way beyond the division between art and thought through a provisional superpositioning of the two that seeks a state and style of exposition irreducible to the fields of art or thought. This "art-thought" takes many names in Laruelle's work—philo-fiction, photo-fiction, art-fiction—but all these clones refer to a "kind of artistic practice" immanent to non-aesthetics that uses the raw materials of art and thought to "perform the art of thought rather than produce a thought about art."[60] The practice of non-aesthetics is determined in the last instance by an axiomatic insistence on the Real as One and as foreclosed to Philosophical Decision by reason of its radical immanence. But it cannot marshal its axiomatic structures into an argument for any specific way of looking or not looking at specific artworks. Nothing in non-aesthetics will determine how to read a specific work of art. What it does decide is *how not to read the relation between art and thought.* Non-aesthetics is a radically abstract practice and a highly creative one. As Galloway astutely observes: "To be sure, the question of nonrepresentationalism in art (namely abstraction) has been around for some time, yet the question of nonrepresentational aesthetics is something quite different."[61] Abstract aesthetics has precedent in the work of Adorno, Benjamin, and Derrida, among others. This tradition has felt it necessary to answer abstract art abstractly by refusing to transcode it back into the regime of representationalism. Laruelle elaborates and extends the tradition of non-representational aesthetics by not only abandoning "age-old questions of reference" but also "reducing aesthetics to a form of fused immanence."[62] The radically immanent and non-representationalist character of Laruelle's non-aesthetics radically distances and distinguishes it from the field of easily "applicable" theories of art or aesthetics.

Is non-aesthetics a theory? Yes, but in a non-standard sense. As we have noted, it will not determine how to read particular artworks although one can provide approximations of non-philosophical readings of art. But, in the last instance, non-aesthetics "displaces the angle of vision" of standard aesthetics. *It is not a theory of art nor of aesthetics, but a theory of their relation.* That "relation," as we have noted, is a theory that postulates a break with the problem of relations between art and aesthetics entirely through a *theory of their relation as non-relationality.* This postulate is in logical conformity with Laruelle's thesis of the Real as One and thus prior to any relation to anything for it is immanent to everything. The radical immanence of the Real as One determines the scope and limits of non-aesthetics. Neither art nor philosophy has the last word. Schemas of prioritization and hierarchal "superstructures" are symptoms of thought's insufficiency to think the radical superposition of art and philosophies as "seen" from the standpoint of "vision-in-One."

We thus have a theory of the relation between art and aesthetics in the form of a general (and abstract) thesis that restates that "relation" as the relation of non-relationality. This theory is a "non-figurative hypothesis" utterly irreducible to any specific instance of philosophy or art. In this sense, Laruelle remains close to the "structural" tradition of thought embodied in the work of Althusser (among others). Non-aesthetics is an extension of the problem of "structural causality" carried out to its most extreme point within the "region" marked as the problem of art and its interpretation. In the articulation of this non-relationality between art and thought, non-aesthetics finds or "discovers" a relative autonomy for *thinking creatively about creativity* whether it be of an aesthetic or theoretical kind. The "theory of non-aesthetics," as a quasi-structural theory of the relation of non-relationality of art to thought, parallels the early Althusser's attempt to carve out a degree of autonomy for theory in the face of calls to *apply* theory. Laruelle's theory resists easy application to reality and it, therefore, parallels the unilaterally determinant force of the Real which escapes every decision and determination.

No theory of art, politics, or otherwise, can have the last word in the last instance on the Real for it is the ultimate precondition of every instance from the first to the last. The Real is prior to even the very concept of "prior" and its causal cognates. Thus, the entire order of standard philosophy (or theory) is entirely reformatted in non-philosophy. There is no question of the priority of the object or the concept. The very question is a "symptom" of the Real that eludes all concepts of causality or any concept in the last instance. The dialectic of art and philosophy or aesthetics is seen from the perspective of "vision-in-One" as a symptomatic splitting of the two that insures the perpetual authority of philosophy over art. But there is neither an "over" nor an "under" operative from the perspective of non-aesthetics. There is only an "in"—in the Real that is One—immanent to the very conditions that make art and thought possible. There is no dialectic, but only a superposition of art and thought whose approximate (but only approximate) and "fictional" signs are given as the clones: "philo-fiction," "art-fiction," or "photo-fiction." The impossible and necessary task of non-aesthetics: to think art without reproducing the decisional cut that this very task necessitates.

The "theory" of non-aesthetics is not then another "theory of aesthetics." It is a clone of standard aesthetic theory or a fiction of standard aesthetics. Its fictional genres constitute superpositions of art and philosophy voided of their decisional impulses. These fictions exceed the limits of expressivity or of commentary. They are neither works of art nor works of commentary: they are clones of each. As Laruelle puts it: the "clone is the transcendental identity which, if we can put it this way, 'is' the Real or is given in its immanent mode but which brings nothing of the real to Real, no predicate, just a function."[63] The clone is a "function" of the Real whereas the "concept" is an effort to determine and decide it. The clone *clones the Real* only insofar as it *clones the Real's non-relationality*. This, as we noted, secures for non-philosophy a relative autonomy inasmuch as that it enters into no relation with the Real in conformity with the axiom that the Real as One is non-relational. So, non-aesthetics secures a relative autonomy from its "objects" and from the Real. Thus, the dialectic between art and philosophy is displaced for a radically "theoretical" discourse that makes no ultimate claim on its objects or on the Real of which it is immanently a part. "Two attitudes are excluded here," writes Laruelle, "a 'critical' and 'aesthetic' commentary on the work and works, but also the very philosophy that always accompany this work."[64] Neither a commentary on the work nor on the stated "philosophy" that consciously or not frames it is taken as the point of departure for non-aesthetics. Rather, the work is a mere "occasion" or a "support" for cloning the relation of art and thought in such a way as to secure the "reciprocal autonomy of art and theory."[65] Non-aesthetics is a "theory" that is neither for nor against aesthetics. It is a "creative" practice that treats art as a "discovery" to be "taken up as a guiding thread . . . to follow the chain of theoretical effects that it sets off in our current knowledge of art . . . and . . . of its spontaneous philosophy. To mark its theoretical effects in excess of all knowledge."[66]

5

Conclusion

Non-aesthetics is an adventure that "sets off" from our "current knowledge of art." But it does not return to art to decide or judge it. It "sets off" for an elsewhere. It is an adventure of theorizing and it is a theory open to research and development. Non-aesthetics is a way of doing things as much as it is a set of axiomatic principles. Non-aesthetics is a radically open-ended practice. But it is not as some critics suggest a theory for which "anything goes." There are parameters. By way of conclusion let us specify what these parameters are and then offer some points of departure for further research and development.

Parameters

The parameters of non-aesthetic theory are metaphysical in nature. Non-philosophy has a metaphysics. Its metaphysical claim is that the Real is immanent and one but foreclosed to full epistemic access. It is true that this is a minimal metaphysics for it does not make any claim on the Real as standard schools of metaphysics do. But the negative claim that the Real is foreclosed to full epistemic access is nonetheless a metaphysical claim for it proclaims (or decides) that the Real is *fundamentally* unknowable as a totality. Laruelle's metaphysical commitments mark his discourse and distinguish it from many others of his generation who (after Heidegger) sought to overcome, deconstruct, or destroy metaphysics. Contrastingly, Laruelle accepts a minimum metaphysical postulate on the Real: the Real is immanent and foreclosed to decisionist finalities. This minimal metaphysical postulate exercises a constraint on non-philosophy's practices, including non-aesthetics. Non-philosophical practice to be non-philosophical must embed this minimal metaphysical constraint into its syntax and structure to be internally consistent and distinguishable from standard philosophy. These metaphysical parameters constrain and define the practice of non-aesthetics.

Non-aesthetics does not explicate art. Rather its style of exposition is marked by art itself. Its aestheticized approach to art and aesthetics takes art and philosophy as a superposed object—and not as an amphibological admixture—that preserves the autonomy of art and thought. Any deviation from these parameters would be inconsistent with non-philosophy's founding metaphysical axiom: the Real is One and foreclosed by virtue of its radical immanence. Non-aesthetics ceases to be non-aesthetics if it decides on the nature of art for art is immanent to the Real which is determinant in the last instance. From the radical perspective of "vision-in-One," the relation between art and philosophy must be rhetorically and syntactically presented as a relation of non-relation since art and thought are both immanent to the Real that is fundamentally non-relational. Now it must be said that this "vision-in-One" is a kind of aspirational vision for one cannot "see" the Real as One according to non-philosophy's core metaphysical axiom. There is no way to practice non-aesthetics (or any other form of non-philosophy) in anything more than an approximate form since no one can practice thought in a rigorously and completely non-relational mode. From our perspective (and not that of the Real) relational thinking is in some measure inescapable. But the defining stylistic character of non-philosophical practice is given in a non-dialectical mode of exposition.

There is then an internal metaphysical consistency to non-philosophical practice that rigorously sets its parameters and distinguishes it from standard philosophies. Fractality, again, provides a useful image for thinking non-philosophy's variety and structural invariance. Non-philosophy can come in many shapes, but like fractals, these "shapes" of non-philosophy are unified by a statistical set of regularities and symmetries. I say this by way of conclusion to to push back against the idea that non-philosophy is a mode of theorizing in which "anything goes." Much can go, but there are rigorous parameters that are ultimately of a metaphysical nature.

With these constraints in mind, I want to suggest some areas for research and development in non-philosophy

Research and development

There are two main areas for future research and development in non-philosophy: *research* into Philosophical Decision and *development* of non-philosophical modes of practice. Research into the mechanics of Philosophical Decision could take the form of a kind of metaphysical reverse engineering to examine how Decision operates and determines a given philosophical World. The implications for theorizing art here are fairly straightforward. Such research would aim at uncovering the metaphysical determinants that engender specific practices of art theory and art criticism. This project is affine with deconstruction. Yet, non-philosophy does not call for the deconstruction of metaphysics, but calls instead to practice metaphysics otherwise. The point would be to force to the fore the metaphysical underpinnings of art theory and criticism in order to have an open metaphysical debate rather than to simply "overcome" metaphysics. The point is not to shame standard aesthetics with the accusation of metaphysics. The point is rather to metaphysically elevate the discussion by openly acknowledging and interrogating the implicit metaphysical commitments that attend established methods and theories of art.

The creative side of the project lies in developing and expanding non-philosophical practices in a unique way. First, it would require constituting new objects for non-philosophical practice. New objects could be constituted by "superposing" a body of criticism, say formalism, and its objects, say Abstract Expressionism. It would then be a matter of taking this theoretical object—formalism-Abstract Expressionism—as a superposed structure with which to think in ways that might have nothing in principle to do with art. To make this clear, let us stay with the same example. It could be that formalism-Abstract Expressionism might enable us to creatively construct a lens of analysis for thinking form, abstraction, and expressivity in areas that have nothing explicitly to do with art as, for example, in politics. This is surely an area for rich development. Non-philosophy has the potential to conjugate or superpose art and philosophy to establish new perspectives on a variety of ways of thinking. There are already signs of this in the work of John O' Maoilearca and Katerina Kolozova who have expanded the study of film and radical philosophy respectively through critical and creative elaborations of non-philosophical practice. These are positive signs of development.

These two areas—critical research and creative development—can profitably open up the field of non-aesthetics beyond explicative work of the sort I have tried to do in this book. But there is also more to do in the way of explication. There are still a number of meta-non-philosophical problems that are in need of clarification. First, a more precise method of reading Laruelle needs to be developed. I am calling here for something like a project of reading Laruelle in the vein of Althusser's project of reading Marx. Not that we should read Laruelle as Althusser read Marx. But it would be worthwhile investigating what new methods of reading might be immanently suggested by Laruelle's own work. To put it simply: we need a method of reading that will not automatically default into an uncritical non-philosophical reading of non-philosophy. Such a method of reading, were it to be discovered or invented, might also prove useful for reading others in addition to Laruelle. Second, we need more clarification on Laruelle's metaphysics. What is the Real for Laruelle really? How is it that the Real is something that can be posited as an axiom, but not known? What conditions the possibility of this very axiom? And could those conditions be explicated through a genealogy of Laruelle's work and his peers? Finally, more research is needed on the ethics of non-philosophy as signified in its resistance to Philosophical Decision. What kind of decisionism is immanent to this resistance? What positive values spring from this very resistance? Research into these questions will help to further clarify non-philosophy's identity and this, in turn, will enable researchers to better see what areas are ripe for further research and development.

Coda

My relation to non-philosophy and non-aesthetics, in particular, has been surprising. From a position of near disdain for Laruelle's texts,

I was won over by their strangeness and the way that they strain the conventions of intelligibility reified by standard philosophical practices. With the renewal of interest in Laruelle within the English-speaking academic community, we are witnessing another French wave of theory very different than that which electrified humanities departments from the 1970s through the late 1990s. Then the great bugbear was metaphysics and systematic thought, but the new wave embraces metaphysics and systematic thought while still remaining committed to the ethos of inclusivity and tolerance enacted under the sign of "philosophies of difference." At a time when jobs in academe are scarce (and very scarce for theorists), younger scholars have taken the courageous step to work on unapologetically deep and transdisciplinary research projects aimed at asking the "big questions" in the face of a university culture in which disciplines have largely retreated into conservative siloes. Anyone who thinks that theory is "dead" need only look beyond those siloes for signs of renewal. Laruelle is part of this renewal and that may be one of the best reasons to read and continue to read his work.

Notes

Preface

1 Laruelle consistently capitalizes the Real for it names the all that is, which is foreclosed to full epistemic access.

2 This term is also capitalized for it is a proper name in Laruelle's non-philosophy.

3 François Laruelle, *Intellectuals and Power, The Insurrection of the Victim: François Laruelle in Conversation with Philippe Petit*, trans. Anthony Paul Smith (Cambridge: Polity Press, 2015), 50.

Chapter 1

1 John O' Maoilearca, "Circumventing the Problem of Initiation: On Introductions to Non-Philosophy," in *Superpositions: Laruelle and the Humanities*, eds. Rocco Gangle and Julius Greve (London: Rowman and Littlefield, 2017).

2 The term "raw material" is used frequently by Laruelle who sees "standard philosophy" as material to be "cloned" by cancelling its ability to decide the Real and thus to put it to novel uses for non-philosophy.

3 Katerina Kolozova, *Towards a Radical Metaphysics of Socialism: Marx and Laruelle* (Brooklyn: Punctum, 2015), 1.

4 Alex Dubilet, "(Non-)Human Identity and Radial Immanence: On Man-in-Person in François Laruelle's Non-Philosophy," in *Superpositions*, 31.

5 John Mullarkey, *Post-Continental Philosophy: An Outline* (London: Continuum, 2006), 137. Note: John Mullarkey now publishes under the name "John O' Maoilearca." Italics in original.

6 Quoted in Robin Mackay, "Introduction: Laruelle Undivided," in François Laruelle, *From Decision to Heresy: Experiments in Non-Standard Thought*, ed. Robin Mackay (Falmouth; New York: Urbanomic/Sequence Press, 2012), 3.

7 Ibid.

8 Richard Rorty, "Philosophy as a Kind of Writing: An Essay on Derrida," *New Literary History*, Vol. 10, No. 1 (1978): 141–60, 144. Italics in original.

9 Leo Steinberg, *Other Criteria: Confrontations with Twentieth-Century Art* (Chicago: The University of Chicago Press, 1972), 88.

10 Ibid.

11 François Laruelle, *Photo-Fiction: A Non-Standard Aesthetics*, trans. Drew S. Burk (Minneapolis: Univocal Publishing, 2012), 63.

12 Quoted in Mackay, "Introduction," 1.

13 Ibid., 8.

14 Ibid.

15 See William James, *Pragmatism: A New Name for Some Old Ways of Thinking* (New York: Floating Press, 2010).

16 Quoted in Mackay, "Introduction," 1–2.

17 Jean Baudrillard, *Forget Foucault* (New York: Semiotext(e), 1987), 10.

18 Ibid., 124.

19 Ibid., 125.

20 Ibid.

21 Quoted in Mackay, "Introduction," 1.

22 Ibid., 10.

23 Ibid.

24 Ibid., 11.

25 Ibid.

26 Ibid., 15.

27 See for example, Cornell West, *Race Matters* (Boston: Beacon Press, 2017).

28 Laruelle, *Intellectuals and Power*, 75.

29 Ibid., 74. Italics in original.

30 The poster went by the name "bmoreed."

31 Mackay, "Introduction," 29.

32 See Jean-François Lyotard, *The Postmodern Condition: A Report on Knowledge*, trans. Geoff Bennington and Brian Massumi (Minneapolis: University of Minnesota Press, 1979).

33 Amelia Jones, *Postmodernism and the En-Gendering of Marcel Duchamp* (Cambridge: Cambridge University Press, 1994), 1.

34 Ibid., 1. Italics in original.

35 Ibid., 10.

36 Dalia Judovitz, *Unpacking Duchamp: Art in Transit* (Berkeley: University of California Press, 1998), 97.

37 O' Maoilearca, "Circumventing the Problem of Initiation," 19.

38 Ibid.

39 Ibid.

40 François Laruelle, *Philosophy and Non-Philosophy*, trans. Taylor Adkins (Minneapolis: Univocal Publishing, 2013), 11.

41 Ibid., 12.

42 Rocco Gangle, *Laruelle's Philosophies of Difference: A Critical Introduction and Guide* (Edinburgh: Edinburgh University Press, 2013), 178. Italics in original.

43 Laruelle, *Philosophy and Non-Philosophy*, 12. Italics in original.

44 Ibid.

45 Anthony Paul Smith, *Laruelle: A Stranger Thought* (Cambridge: Polity, 2016), 60.

46 Quoted in Smith, *Laruelle*, 61.

47 Ibid., 63.

48 Smith, *Laruelle*, 63.

49 Ibid., 37.

50 Ibid.

51 See Andrew Feenberg, *The Philosophy of Praxis: Marx, Lukács, and the Frankfurt School* (New York; London: Verso, 2014).

52 François Laruelle, *The Concept of Non-Photography*, trans. Robin Mackay (New York: Urbanomic/Sequence Press, 2011), 29.

53 Gilles Deleuze, *Pure Immanence: A Life*, trans. Anne Boyman (New York: Zone Books, 2001), 30–31.

54 Laruelle, *Philosophy and Non-Philosophy*, 17–18. Italics in original.

55 Italics in original. Alexander R. Galloway, *Superpositions*, October 11, 2014. http://cultureandcommunication.org/galloway/super positions.

56 Laruelle, *Philosophy and Non-Philosophy*, 17.

57 O' Maoilearca, "Circumventing the Problem of Initiation," 20.

Chapter 2

1 Julia Margaret Cameron, "Annals of My Glass House," in *Photography in Print: 1816 to the Present*, ed. Vicki Goldberg (Albuquerque: University of New Mexico Press, 1981), 182.

2 Quoted in Victoria Olsen, *From Life: Julia Margaret Cameron and Victorian Photography* (New York: Palgrave Macmillan, 2003), 155.

3 Roland Barthes, *Camera Lucida: Reflections on Photography*, trans. Richard Howard (New York: Hill and Wang, 2010), 92.

4 My insights here are indebted to the work of Lindsay Smith. See Smith, "The Politics of Focus," in *Photographic Theory: A Historical Anthology*, ed. Andrew Hershberger (Malden: Wiley-Blackwell, 2015).

5 See Andrew Hass, *Hegel and the Art of Negation* (London: I. B. Tauris, 2014).

6 Ibid., 11.

7 Quoted in Olsen, *From Life*, 166.

8 Smith, "The Politics of Focus," 361.

9 Hass, *Hegel and the Art of Negation*, 14.

10 Ibid.

11 Smith, *Laruelle*, 36.

12 See Martin Jay, *Adorno* (Cambridge: Harvard University Press, 1984).

13 Theodor Adorno, *Aesthetic Theory*, trans. Robert Hullot-Kentor (Minneapolis: University of Minnesota Press, 1997), 1.

14 Geoff Boucher, *Adorno Reframed: Interpreting Key Thinkers for the Arts* (London: I. B. Tauris, 2013), 106.

15 Ibid., 108.

16 Robert Hullot-Kentor, "Translator's Introduction," in Adorno, *Aesthetic Theory*, xi.

17 Ibid., xi–xii.

18 Laruelle, *The Concept of Non-Photography*, 8.

19 Walter Benjamin, "On the Concept of History," in *Walter Benjamin: Selected Writings, Volume 4, 1938-1940*, trans. Edmund Jephcott and Others (Cambridge: Belknap Press, 2006), 390.

20 Ibid.

21 Ibid.

22 Ibid.

23 Richard Wolin, *Walter Benjamin: An Aesthetic of Redemption* (New York: Columbia University Press, 1982), 124.

24 Ibid.

25 Laruelle, *Photo-Fiction*, 7.

26 Martin Jay, *The Dialectical Imagination: A History of the Frankfurt School and the Institute of Social Research, 1923-1950* (Berkeley: University of California Press, 1996), 175–76.

27 Laruelle, *The Concept of Non-Photography*, 70.

28 Jacques Derrida, "Cartouches," in *The Truth in Painting*, trans. Geoff Bennington and Ian McLeod (Chicago: The University of Chicago Press, 1987), 188.

29 Ibid., 189.

30 Ibid., 191.

31 David Wills, "Lemming," in *Matchbook: Essays in Deconstruction* (Stanford: Stanford University Press, 2005), 35.

32 See Clement Greenberg, "Modernist Painting," in *Art in Theory, 1900-2000: An Anthology of Changing Ideas*, eds. Charles Harrison and Paul Wood (Malden: Blackwell Publishing, 2003), 773–79.

33 Jacques Rancière, "Painting in the Text," in *The Future of the Image*, trans. Gregory Elliott (London: Verso, 2009), 75–76.

34 Ibid., 78.

35 Gregory L. Ulmer, "The Object of Post-Criticism," in *The Anti-Aesthetic: Essays on Postmodern Culture*, ed. Hal Foster (Port Townsend: Bay Press, 1983), 83.

36 François Laruelle, *Principles of Non-Philosophy*, trans. Nicola Rubczak and Anthony Paul Smith (London: Bloomsbury, 2013), 32.

37 Anthony Paul Smith, *François Laruelle's* Principles of Non-Philosophy: *A Critical Introduction and Guide* (Edinburgh: University of Edinburgh Press, 2016), 83.

38 John O' Maoilearca, *All Thoughts Are Equal: Laruelle and Nonhuman Philosophy* (Minneapolis: University of Minnesota Press, 2015), 173.

39 Ibid., 175.

40 See Laruelle, *The Concept of Non-Photography*, especially chapter 2.

41 Ibid., 56.

42 Ibid., 25.

43 Ibid., 18.

44 Homi Bhabha, "Elusive Objects: Anish Kapoor's Fissionary Art," in *Anish Kapoor* (London: The Royal Academy of Arts, 2009), 26.

45 Laruelle, *The Concept of Non-Photography*, 69–70.

46 Ibid., 70.

47 Rocco Gangle and Julius Greve, "Introduction: Superposing Non-Standard Philosophy and Humanities Discourse," in *Superpositions*, 3.

48 Laruelle, *The Concept of Non-Photography*, 70–71.

49 Ibid., 70.

50 Theodor Adorno, *Negative Dialectics*, trans. E. B. Ashton (New York: Continuum, 1973), 33 (my emphasis).

51 Ibid.

52 Ibid.

53 Jonathan Culler, *The Literary in Theory* (Stanford: Stanford University Press, 2007), 39.

54 Laruelle, *Philosophy and Non-Philosophy*, 227.

55 Ibid.

56 Ibid., 229.

57 Walter Benjamin, *The Arcades Project*, trans. Howard Eiland and Kevin McLaughlin (Cambridge: Belknap/Harvard University Press, 1999), 459.

58 Theodor Adorno, *Minima Moralia: Reflections from Damaged Life*, trans. E. F. N. Jephcott (London: Verso, 2005), 247.

59 See Theodor Adorno and Max Horkheimer, *Towards a New Manifesto*, trans. Rodney Livingstone (London: Verso, 2011).

60 Walter Benjamin, "Surrealism: The Last Snapshot of the European Intelligentsia," in *Selected Writings, Volume 2, Part 1, 1927-1930*, eds. Michael W. Jennings, Howard Eiland, and Gary Smith, trans. Rodney Livingstone and Others (Cambridge: Belknap/Harvard University Press, 1999), 240.

61 See Hannah Arendt, *Eichmann in Jerusalem: A Report on the Banality of Evil* (New York: Penguin, 2006).

62 Adorno, *Minima Moralia*, 247.

63 Ibid.

64 Laruelle, *Photo-Fiction*, 5.

65 Ibid.

66 Ibid., 23.

67 Alexander R. Galloway, *Laruelle: Against the Digital* (Minneapolis: University of Minnesota Press, 2014), 158.

68 Ibid.

69 Ibid.

70 Ibid., 159.

71 Ibid.

72 Laruelle, *Photo-Fiction*, 3.

73 Ibid.

74 Ibid., 3–4.

75 Ibid., 4.

76 Ibid.

77 Ibid., 5.

78 Homi K. Bhabha, *The Location of Culture* (London: Routledge, 1994), 53.

79 See Bhabha, *The Location of Culture*. This term used throughout.

80 Smith, *Laruelle*, 122.

81 Ibid.

82 Ibid., 119.

83 Ibid., 120.

Chapter 3

1 Michael Frayn, C*openhagen* (New York: Anchor Books, 1998), 92.

2 Frayn, "Postscript," in *Copenhagen*, 95.

3 Ibid.

4 Ibid., 97.

5 Ibid., 96.

6 Quoted in Frayn, "Postscript," 96–97.

7 Frayn, "Postscript," 97.

8 Frayn, *Copenhagen*, 25.

9 Ibid., 8.

10 Ibid., 4.

11 Ibid.

12 Ibid., 53.

13 Ibid., 92.

14 Ibid., 86.

15 Ibid., 94.

16 Smith, *Laruelle*, 49.

17 See Walter Benjamin, "The Work of Art in the Age of Its Technological Reproducibility," in *The Work of Art in the Age of Its Technological Reproducibility and Other Writings on Media*, trans. Michael Jennings (Cambridge: Belknap/Harvard University Press, 2008).

18 Quoted in Smith, *Laruelle*, 123.

19 Keith Tilford, "Generalized Transformations and Technologies of Investigation: Laruelle, Art, and the Scientific Model," in *Superpositions*, 145.

20 Smith, *Laruelle*, 123.

21 Ibid., 124.

22 Laruelle, *Photo-Fiction*, 28.

23 See Steinberg, *Other Criteria*.

24 See Arkady Plotnitsky, *Complementarity: Anti-Epistemology After Bohr and Derrida* (Durham: Duke University Press, 1994).

25 Quoted in Tilford, "Generalized Transformations and Technologies of Investigations," 144.

26 Tilford, "Generalized Transformations and Technologies of Investigations," 144.

27 Laruelle, *Photo-Fiction*, 12.

28 Ibid., 12–13.

29 Ibid., 63.

30 Ibid., 55.

31 Ibid., 63.

32 Ibid.

33 Tilford, "Generalized Transformations and Technologies of Investigations," 149.

34 Ibid., 149.

35 Galloway, *Laruelle*, 120.

36 Ibid., 120–21.

37 François Laruelle, *Introduction to Non-Marxism,* trans. Anthony Paul Smith (Minneapolis: Univocal Publishing, 2015), 10.

38 Ibid.

39 Ibid., 36.

40 Ibid. Italics in original.

41 Kolozova, *Towards a Radical Metaphysics of Socialism*, 2.

42 I owe an enormous debt to the work of Gregory Elliot whose book on Althusser was the first book I read when I was studying for my doctorate. It remains indispensable to me. See Gregory Elliott, *Althusser: The Detour of Theory* (Chicago: Haymarket Books, 2009).

43 Louis Althusser, *Philosophy and the Spontaneous Philosophy of the Scientists and Other Essays*, ed. Gregory Elliott, trans. Ben Brewster, James H. Kavanagh, Thomas E. Lewis, Grahame Lock, and Warren Montag (London: Verso, 2011), 13.

44 Althusser, *Philosophy and the Spontaneous Philosophy of the Scientists*, 7. Italics in original.

45 Ibid., 14.

46 Ibid. Italics in original.

47 Ibid., 56.

48 Ibid., 15. Italics in original.

49 The term "auto-position" is Laruelle's. It appears throughout his work. It refers to the process by which Philosophical Decision "automatically" positions a discourse within its logic.

50 I am making use of the concept of "symptomatic reading" that Althusser pioneered in *Reading Capital*. See Louis Althusser and Étienne Balibar, *Reading Capital*, trans. Ben Brewster (London; New York: Verso, 2009).

51 Alain Badiou, "The Althusserian Definition of 'Theory'," in *The Concept in Crisis: Reading Capital Today*, ed. Nick Nesbitt (Durham; London: Duke University Press, 2017), 26.

52 Ibid.

53 Ibid.

54 Ibid. Italics in original.

55 Ibid.

56 Laruelle, *Introduction to Non-Marxism*, 34.

57 Ibid., 36. Italics in original.

58 Ibid., 37.

59 Ibid., 3.

60 Ibid., 68.

61 Ibid.

62 Ibid.

63 Kolozova, *Towards a Radical Metaphysics of Socialism*, 14.

64 The claim that there is no such thing as Marxist philosophy is made by Balibar. See Étienne Balibar, *The Philosophy of Marx*, trans. Gregory Elliot and Chris Turner (London; New York: Verso, 2017).

65 Laruelle, *Introduction to Non-Marxism*, 76.

66 Ibid.

67 O' Maoilearca, *All Thoughts are Equal*, 133. Italics in original.

68 Frayn, "Postscript," 97.

69 Laruelle, *Introduction to Non-Marxism*, 79.

70 Smith, *Laruelle*, 37.

71 Laruelle, *The Concept of Non-Photography*, 78.

72 Laruelle, *Photo-Fiction*, 1.

73 Laruelle, *The Concept of Non-Photography*, 1.

74 Laruelle, *Photo-Fiction*, 61.

75 Benjamin, *The Arcades Project*, 459.

76 François Laruelle, *Dictionary of Non-Philosophy*, trans. Taylor Adkins (Minneapolis: Univocal Publishing, 2013), 78.

77 Ibid., 79.

78 Ibid.

79 Gangle and Greve, "Introduction," 2. Italics in original.

80 Laruelle, *Dictionary of Non-Philosophy*, 142.

81 Kolozova, *Towards a Radical Metaphysics of Socialism*, 31.

82 Ibid., 37.

Chapter 4

1 Laruelle, *Introduction to Non-Marxism*, 85.

2 Laruelle, *Dictionary of Non-Philosophy*, 64.

3 Smith, *Laruelle*, 47.

4 Laruelle, *Philosophy and Non-Philosophy*, 9. Italics in original.

5 See Baudrillard, *Forget Foucault*.

6 See Julius Greve, "The Decisional Apparatus," in *Superpositions*.

7 Smith, *Laruelle*, 25.

8 Joseph Kosuth, "Art After Philosophy," in *Art in Theory, 1900-2000*, 856. Italics in original.

9 Ibid., 857.

10 Bhabha, "Elusive Objects," 25–26.

11 Ibid., 26.

12 Ibid., 27. Italics in original.

13 See Donna Haraway, *Simians, Cyborgs, and Women: The Reinvention of Nature* (London: Routledge, 1990).

14 Benjamin, *The Arcades Project*, 459.

15 Ibid.

16 See Christopher Langlois, *Samuel Beckett and the Terror of Literature* (Edinburgh: University of Edinburgh Press, 2017).

17 Ibid., 41.

18 Laruelle, *Photo-Fiction*, 1.

19 J. Fiona Ragheb, "Of Situations and Sites," in *Dan Flavin: The Architecture of Light* (New York: Guggenheim Museum Publications, 1999), 15.

20 Ibid.

21 Ibid.

22 Ibid., 14.

23 Ibid.

24 Ibid.

25 Stephen Eric Bronner, *Modernism at the Barricades: Aesthetics, Politics, Utopia* (New York: Columbia University Press, 2012), 115.

26 I am here in agreement with Georg Lukács general line of argument that a true socialist realism would have to present the "social" as a dynamic process and the static, freeze-frame aesthetics of post-Leninist, official art failed to realistically represent this essential aspect of the social as a historical and dynamic process.

27 See Martin Jay, *Downcast Eyes: The Denigration of Vision in Twentieth-Century French Thought* (Berkley: University of California Press, 1993).

28 Laruelle, *The Concept of Non-Photography*, 5.

29 See Michael Fried, "Art and Objecthood," in *Art and Objecthood: Essays and Reviews* (Chicago: The University of Chicago Press, 1998).

30 Laruelle has written on Turrell's prints titled, *First Light*. I do draw on some of his ideas presented in that essay, but I transpose them into my discussion of Turrell's projection work.

31 See Robert Morris, "Notes on Sculpture," in *Art in Theory, 1900-2000*.

32 Craig Adcock, *James Turrell: The Art of Light and Space* (Berkeley: University of California Press, 1990), 12.

33 Laruelle, *Philosophy and Non-Philosophy*, 91–92.

34 Smith, *Laruelle*, 45.

35 Ibid.

36 Adcock, *James Turrell*, 1–2.

37 Ibid., 13.

38 Quoted in Galloway, *Laruelle*, 154. Italics in original.

39 Galloway, *Laruelle*, 154.

40 Ibid., 155.

41 Ibid. Italics in original.

42 Laruelle, *Philosophy and Non-Philosophy*, 56. Italics in original.

43 Laruelle, *Dictionary of Non-Philosophy*, 49–50.

44 Quoted in Louis Althusser, "Contradiction and Overdetermination," in *For Marx*, trans. Ben Brewster (New York: Vintage Books, 1970), 111.

45 Ibid., 112.

46 Ibid., 113. Italics in original.

47 Ted Benton, *The Rise and Fall of Structural Marxism: Althusser and His Influence* (New York: St. Martin's Press, 1984), 64. Italics in original.

48 Laruelle, *Introduction to Non-Marxism*, 41.

49 Ibid.

50 Ibid., 49.

51 Ibid., 46.

52 Ibid.

53 Laruelle uses the term "infrastructure" rather than "superstructure" in order to distinguish his immanent (flat) ontology from the dyadic architectonic of classical Marxism.

54 Laruelle, *Introduction to Non-Marxism*, 51.

55 Ibid.

56 Smith, *Laruelle*, 44.

57 Galloway, *Laruelle*, 155. Italics in original.

58 Laruelle, *Introduction to Non-Marxism*, 141.

59 Smith, *Laruelle*, 74.

60 Ibid., 122.

61 Galloway, *Laruelle*, 164.

62 Ibid., 165.

63 Laruelle, *Principles of Non-Philosophy*, 30.

64 Laruelle, *The Concept of Non-Photography*, 69.

65 Ibid., 70.

66 Ibid., 70–71.

Index